The Collected Poems of
Rupert Brooke

RUPERT BROOKE

Born at Rugby, August 3, 1887
Fellow of King's College, Cambridge, 1913
Sub-Lieutenant, R.N.V.R., September, 1914
Antwerp Expedition, October, 1914
Sailed with British Mediterranean Expeditionary Force,
February 28, 1915
Died in the Ægean, April 23, 1915

Rupert Brooke

1914

THE COLLECTED POEMS
OF
RUPERT BROOKE

WITH AN INTRODUCTION

by

GEORGE EDWARD WOODBERRY

AND A BIOGRAPHICAL NOTE
BY MARGARET LAVINGTON

With Frontispiece

DODD, MEAD & COMPANY
NEW YORK - 1969

PRINTED IN THE UNITED STATES OF AMERICA
BY THE VAIL-BALLOU PRESS, INC., BINGHAMTON, N. Y.

INTRODUCTION

Rupert Brooke was both fair to see and winning in his ways. There was at the first contact both bloom and charm; and most of all there was life. To use the word his friends describe him by, he was "vivid." This vitality, though manifold in expression, is felt primarily in his sensations—surprise mingled with delight—

"One after one, like tasting a sweet food."

This is life's "first fine rapture." It makes him patient to name over those myriad things (each of which seems like a fresh discovery) curious but potent, and above all common, that he "loved,"—he the "Great Lover." Lover of what, then? Why, of

"White plates and cups clean-gleaming,
Ringed with blue lines,"—

and the like, through thirty lines of exquisite words; and he is captivated by the multiple brevity of these vignettes of sense, keen, momentary, ecstatic with the morning dip of youth in the wonderful stream. The poem is a catalogue of vital sensations and "dear names" as well. "All these have been my loves."

The spring of these emotions is the natural body, but it sends pulsations far into the spirit. The feeling rises in direct

[5]

observation, but it is soon aware of the "outlets of the sky." He sees objects practically unrelated, and links them in strings; or he sees them pictorially; or, he sees pictures immersed as it were in an atmosphere of thought. When the process is complete, the thought suggests the picture and is its origin. Then the Great Lover revisits the bottom of the monstrous world, and imaginatively and thoughtfully recreates that strange undersea, whose glooms and gleams and muds are well known to him as a strong and delighted swimmer; or, at the last, drifts through the dream of a South Sea lagoon, still with a philosophical question in his mouth. Yet one can hardly speak of "completion." These are real first flights. What we have in this volume is not so much a work of art as an artist in his birth trying the wings of genius.

The poet loves his new-found element. He clings to mortality; to life, not thought; or, as he puts it, to the concrete,—let the abstract "go pack!" "There's little comfort in the wise," he ends. But in the unfolding of his precocious spirit, the literary control comes uppermost; his boat, finding its keel, swings to the helm of mind. How should it be otherwise for a youth well-born, well-bred, in college air? Intellectual primacy showed itself to him in many wandering "loves," fine lover that he was; but in the end he was an intellectual lover, and the magnet seems to have been especially powerful in the ghosts of the men of "wit," Donne, Marvell—erudite lords of language, poets in another world than ours, a less "ample ether," a less "divine air," our fathers thought, but poets of "eternity." A quintessential drop of intellect is apt to be in poetic blood. How Platonism fascinates the poets, like a shining bait! Rupert Brooke will have none of it; but at a turn of the verse he is back at it, examining, tasting, refusing. In those alternate drives of the thought in his South Sea idyl (clever as tennis play) how he slips from phenomenon to idea and reverses, happy with either, it seems, "were t'other dear charmer away." How bravely he tries to free himself from the cling of earth, at the close of the "Great Lover!" How little he succeeds! His muse knew only earthly tongues,—so far as he understood.

Why this persistent cling to mortality,—with its quick-coming cry against death and its heaped anathemas on the transformations of decay? It is the old story once more:— the vision of the first poets, the world that "passes away." The poetic eye of Keats saw it,—

> "Beauty that must die,
> And Joy whose hand is ever at his lips
> Bidding adieu."

The reflective mind of Arnold meditated it,—

> "the world that seems
> To lie before us like a land of dreams,
> So various, so beautiful, so new,
> Hath really neither joy, nor love, nor light,
> Nor certitude, nor peace, nor help for pain."—

So Rupert Brooke,—

> "But the best I've known
> Stays here, and changes, breaks, grows old, is blown
> About the winds of the world, and fades from brains
> Of living men, and dies.
> Nothing remains."

And yet,—

> "Oh, never a doubt but somewhere I shall wake;"

again,—

[7]

>   "the light,
> Returning, shall give back the golden hours,
> Ocean a windless level. . . ."

again, best of all, in the last word,—

> "Still may Time hold some golden space
>   Where I'll unpack that scented store
> Of song and flower and sky and face,
>   And count, and touch, and turn them o'er,
>   Musing upon them."

He cannot forego his sensations, that "box of compacted sweets." He even forefeels a ghostly landscape where two shall go wandering through the night, "alone." So the faith that broke its chrysalis in the first disillusionment of boyhood, in "Second Best," beautiful with the burden of Greek lyricism, ends triumphant with the spirit still unsubdued.—

> "Proud, then, clear-eyed and laughing, go to greet
> Death as a friend."

So go, "with unreluctant tread." But in the disillusionment of beauty and of love there is an older tone. With what bitter savor, with what grossness of diction, caught from the Elizabethan and satirical elements in his culture, he spends anger in words! He reacts, he rebels, he storms. A dozen poems hardly exhaust his gall. It is not merely that beauty and joy and love are transient, now, but in their going they are corrupted into their opposites,—ugliness, pain, indifference. And his anger once stilled by speech, what lassitude follows!

Life, in this volume, is hardly less evident by its ecstasy than by its collapse. It is a book of youth, sensitive, vigorous, sound; but it is the fruit of intensity, and bears the traits.

[8]

The search for solitude, the relief from crowds, the open door into nature; the sense of flight and escape; the repeated thought of safety, the insistent fatigue, the cry for sleep;—all these bear confession in their faces. "Flight," "Town and Country," "The Voice," are eloquent of what they leave untold; and the climax of "Retrospect,"—

"And I should sleep, and I should sleep,"—

or the sestet of "Waikiki," or the whole fainting sonnet entitled "A Memory," belong to the nadir of vitality. At moments weariness set in like a spiritual tide. I associate, too, with such moods, psychologically at least, his visions of the "arrested moment," as in "Dining Room Tea,"—a sort of trance state—or in the pendant sonnet. Analogous moods are not infrequent in the great poets. Rupert Brooke seems to have faltered, nervously, at times; these poems mirror faithfully such moments. But even when the image of life, imaginative or real, falters so, how essentially vital it still is, and clothed in an exquisite body of words like the traditional "rainbow hues of the dying fish!" For I cannot express too strongly my admiration of the literary sense of this young poet, and my delight in it. "All these have been my loves," he says, if I may repeat the phrase; but he seems to have loved the words, as much as the things,—"dear names," he adds. The born man of letters speaks there. So, when his pulse is at its lowest, he cannot forget the beautiful surface of his South Sea idyls or of versified English gardens and lanes. He cared as much for the expression as for the thing, which is what makes a man of letters. So fixed is this habit that his art, truly, is independent of his bodily estate. In his poems of "collapse" as in those of "ecstasy" he seems to me equally master of his mood,—like those poets who are "for all time." His literary skill in verse was ripe, how long so ever he might have to live.

II

To come, then, to art, which is above personality, what of that? Art is, at most, but the mortal relic of genius; yet it is true of that, like Ozymandias' statue, "nothing beside remains." Rupert Brooke was already perfected in verbal and stylistic execution. He might have grown in variety, richness and significance, in scope and in detail, no doubt; but as an artisan in metrical words and pauses, he was past apprenticeship. He was still a restless experimenter, but in much he was a master. In the brief stroke of description, which he inherited from his early attachment to the concrete; in the rush of words, especially verbs; in the concatenation of objects, the flow of things *en masse* through his verse, still with the impulse of "the bright speed" he had at the source; in his theatrical impersonation of abstractions, as in "The Funeral of Youth," where for once the abstract and the concrete are happily fused;—in all these there are the elements, and in the last there is the perfection, of mastery. For one thing, he knew how to end. It is with him a dramatic secret. The brief stroke does this work time and time again in his verse, nowhere better than in "at dead *Youth's* funeral": all were there,—

"All, except only *Love*—*Love* had died long ago."

The poem is like a vision of an old time *Masque*:—

"The sweet lad *Rhyme*"——
"*Ardour*, the sunlight on his greying hair"——
"*Beauty* . . . pale in her black; dry-eyed, she stood alone."

[10]

How vivid! The lines owe something to his eye for costume, for staging; but, as mere picture writing, it is as firm as if carved on an obelisk. And as he reconciled concrete and abstract here; so he had left his short breath, in those earlier lines, behind, and had come into the long sweep and open water of great style:—

> "And light on waving grass, he knows not when,
> And feet that ran, but where, he cannot tell."

Or;—

> "And feel, who have laid our groping hands away;
> And see, no longer blinded by our eyes,"

Or, more briefly,—

> "In wise majestic melancholy train."

And this,—

> "And evening hush broken by homing wings,"

Such lines as these, apart from their beauty, are in the best manner of English poetic style. So, in many minor ways, he shuffled contrast and climax, and the like, adept in the handling of poetic rhetoric that he had come to be; but in three ways he was conspicuously successful in his art.

The first of these—they are all in the larger forms of art—is the dramatic sonnet, by which I do not mean merely a sonnet in dialogue or advancing by simple contrast; but one in which there may be these things, but also there is a tragic reversal or its equivalent. Not to consider it too curiously, take "The Hill." This sonnet is beautiful in action and diction; its eloquence speeds it on with a lift; the situation is the very crest of life; then,—

"We shall go down with unreluctant tread,
Rose-crowned into the darkness! . . . Proud we were,
And laughed, that had such brave true things to say.
—And then you suddenly cried and turned away."

The dramatic sonnet in English has not gone beyond that, for beauty, for brevity, for tragic effect,—nor, I add, for unspoken loyalty to reality. Reality was, perhaps, what he most dearly wished for; here he achieved it. In many another sonnet he won the laurel; but if I were to venture to choose, it is in the dramatic handling of the sonnet that he is most individual and characteristic.

The second great success of his genius, formally considered, lay in the narrative idyl, either in the Miltonic way of flashing bits of English country landscape before the eye, as in "Grantchester," or by applying essentially the same method to the water world of fishes or the South Sea world, both on a philosophic background. These are all master poems of a kaleidoscopic beauty and charm, where the brief pictures play in and out of a woven veil of thought, irony, mood, with a delightful intellectual pleasuring. He thoroughly enjoys doing the poetical magic. Such bits of English retreats or Pacific paradises, so full of idyllic charm, exquisite in image and movement, are among the rarest of poetic treasures. The thought of Milton and of Marvell only adds an old world charm to the most modern of the works of the Muses. What lightness of touch, what ease of movement, what brilliancy of hue! What vivacity throughout! Even in "Retrospect," what actuality!

And the third success is what I should call the "mélange." That is, the method of indiscrimination by which he gathers up experience, and pours it out again in language, with full disregard of its relative values. His good taste saves him from what in another would be shipwreck, but this indifference to values, this apparent lack of selection in material, while at times it gives a huddled flow, more than anything else "modernizes" the verse. It yields, too, an effect of abundant vitality, and it makes facile the change from grave to gay and the like. The "mélange," as I call it, is rather an innovation in English verse, and to be found only rarely. It exists, however; and especially it was dear to Keats in his youth. It is by excellent taste, and by style, that the poet here overcomes its early difficulties.

In these three formal ways, besides in minor matters, it appears to me that Rupert Brooke, judged by the most orthodox standards, had succeeded in poetry.

III

But in his first notes, if I may indulge my private taste, I find more of the intoxication of the god. These early poems are the lyrical cries and luminous flares of a dawn, no doubt; but they are incarnate of youth. Capital among them is "Blue Evening." It is original and complete. In its whispering embraces of sense, in the terror of seizure of the spirit, in the tranquil euthanasia of the end by the touch of speechless beauty, it seems to me a true symbol of life whole and entire. It is beautiful in language and feeling, with an extraordinary clarity and rise of power; and, above all, though rare in experience, it is real. A young poet's poem; but it has a quality never captured by perfect art. A poem for poets, no doubt; but that is the best kind. So, too, the poem, entitled "Sleeping Out," charms me and stirs me with its golden clangors and crying flames of emotion as it mounts up to "the white one flame," to "the laughter and the lips of light." It is like a holy Italian picture,—remote, inaccessible, alone. The "white flame" seems to have had a mystic meaning to the boy; it occurs repeatedly. And another poem,—not to make too long a story of my private enthusiasms—"Ante Aram,"—wakes all my classical blood,—

> "voice more sweet than the far plaint of viols is,
> Or the soft moan of any grey-eyed lute player,"

But these things are *arcana*.

IV

There is a grave in Scyros, amid the white and pinkish marble of the isle, the wild thyme and the poppies, near the green and blue waters. There Rupert Brooke was buried. Thither have gone the thoughts of his countrymen, and the hearts of the young especially. It will long be so. For a new star shines in the English heavens.

G. E.W.

Beverly, Mass., October, 1915.

CONTENTS

1905–1908

Introduction 5
Second Best 21
Day That I Have Loved 23
Sleeping Out: Full Moon 25
In Examination 26
Pine-Trees and the Sky: Evening 27
Wagner 28
The Vision of the Archangels 29
Seaside 30
On the Death of Smet-Smet, the Hippopotamus-Goddess 31
The Song of the Pilgrims 33
The Song of the Beasts 35
Failure 37
Ante Aram 38
Dawn 39
The Call 40
The Wayfarers 42
The Beginning 43

1908–1911

Sonnet:
   "Oh! Death will find me, long before I tire" 47
Sonnet:
   "I said I splendidly loved you; it's not true" . . . 48
Success 49
Dust 50
Kindliness 52
Mummia 54
The Fish 56
Thoughts on the Shape of the Human Body . . . 59
Flight 60
The Hill 62
The One Before the Last 63
The Jolly Company 65
The Life Beyond 66

Lines Written in the Belief That the Ancient Roman
  Festival of the Dead Was Called Ambarvalia . . . 67
Dead Men's Love 70
Town and Country 71
Paralysis 73
Menelaus and Helen 74
Libido 75
Jealousy 76
Blue Evening 78
The Charm 80
Finding 81
Song 83
The Voice 84
Dining-Room Tea 86
The Goddess in the Wood 89
A Channel Passage 90
Victory 91
Day and Night 92

EXPERIMENTS

Choriambics—I 95
Choriambics—II 96
Desertion 98

1914

  I   Peace 101
 II   Safety 102
III   The Dead 103
IV   The Dead 104
 V   The Soldier 105
The Treasure 106

THE SOUTH SEAS

Tiare Tahiti 109
Retrospect 112
The Great Lover 114
Heaven 117
Doubts 119
[16]

There's Wisdom in Women 120
He Wonders Whether to Praise or to Blame Her . . 121
A Memory (*From a sonnet-sequence*) 122
One Day 123
Waikiki 124
Hauntings 125
Sonnet (*Suggested by some of the Proceedings of the
    Society for Psychical Research*) 126
Clouds 127
Mutability 128

OTHER POEMS

The Busy Heart 131
Love 132
Unfortunate 133
The Chilterns 134
Home 136
The Night Journey 137
Song 139
Beauty and Beauty 140
The Way That Lovers Use 141
Mary and Gabriel 142
The Funeral of Youth: Threnody 144

GRANTCHESTER

The Old Vicarage, Grantchester (*Café des Westens,
    Berlin, May, 1912*) 149
Fafaïa 154

APPENDIX

Fragment 157
The Dance 158
Song 159
Sometimes Even Now 160
Sonnet: In Time of Revolt 161
A Letter to a Live Poet 162
Fragment on Painters 164
The True Beatitude 165

Sonnet Reversed 166
It's Not Going to Happen Again 167
The Little Dog's Day 168
Rupert Brooke (A Biographical Note) 170

1905--1908

SECOND BEST

HERE in the dark, O heart;
Alone with the enduring Earth, and Night,
And Silence, and the warm strange smell of clover;
Clear-visioned, though it break you; far apart
From the dead best, the dear and old delight;
Throw down your dreams of immortality,
O faithful, O foolish lover!
Here's peace for you, and surety; here the one
Wisdom—the truth!—"All day the good glad sun
Showers love and labour on you, wine and song;
The greenwood laughs, the wind blows, all day long
Till night." And night ends all things.
                            Then shall be
No lamp relumed in heaven, no voices crying,
Or changing lights, or dreams and forms that hover!
(And, heart, for all your sighing,
Then gladness and those tears are over, over. . . .)

And has the truth brought no new hope at all,
Heart, that you're weeping yet for Paradise?
Do they still whisper, the old weary cries?
" 'Mid youth and song, feasting and carnival,
Through laughter, through the roses, as of old
Comes Death, on shadowy and relentless feet,
Death, unappeasable by prayer or gold;
Death is the end, the end!"
Proud, then, clear-eyed and laughing, go to greet
Death as a friend!

Exile of immortality, strongly wise,
Strain through the dark with undesirous eyes
To what may lie beyond it. Sets your star,
O heart, for ever! Yet, behind the night,
Waits for the great unborn, somewhere afar,
Some white tremendous daybreak. And the light,
Returning, shall give back the golden hours,
Ocean a windless level, Earth a lawn
Spacious and full of sunlit dancing-places,
And laughter, and music, and, among the flowers,
The gay child-hearts of men, and the child-faces
O heart, in the great dawn!

DAY THAT I HAVE LOVED

TENDERLY, day that I have loved, I close your eyes,
   And smooth your quiet brow, and fold your thin dead hands.
The grey veils of the half-light deepen; colour dies.
   I bear you, a light burden, to the shrouded sands,

Where lies your waiting boat, by wreaths of the sea's making
   Mist-garlanded, with all grey weeds of the water crowned.
There you'll be laid, past fear of sleep or hope of waking;
   And over the unmoving sea, without a sound,

Faint hands will row you outward, out beyond our sight,
   Us with stretched arms and empty eyes on the far-gleaming
And marble sand. . . .
        Beyond the shifting cold twilight,
   Further than laughter goes, or tears, further than dreaming,

There'll be no port, no dawn-lit islands! But the drear
   Waste darkening, and, at length, flame ultimate on the
   deep.
Oh, the last fire—and you, unkissed, unfriended there!
   Oh, the long way's red ending, and we not there to weep!

(We found you pale and quiet, and strangely crowned with
   flowers,
   Lovely and secret as a child. You came with us,
Came happily, hand in hand with the young dancing hours,
   High on the downs at dawn!) Void now and tenebrous,

The grey sands curve before me. . . .
        From the inland meadows,
Fragrant of June and clover, floats the dark, and fills
The hollow sea's dead face with little creeping shadows,
    And the white silence brims the hollow of the hills.

Close in the nest is folded every weary wing,
    Hushed all the joyful voices; and we, who held you dear,
Eastward we turn and homeward, alone, remembering . . .
    Day that I loved, day that I loved, the Night is here!

SLEEPING OUT: FULL MOON

THEY sleep within. . . .
I cower to the earth, I waking, I only.
High and cold thou dreamest, O queen, high-dreaming and
    lonely.

We have slept too long, who can hardly win
The white one flame, and the night-long crying;
The viewless passers; the world's low sighing
With desire, with yearning,
To the fire unburning,
To the heatless fire, to the flameless ecstasy! . . .

Helpless I lie.
And around me the feet of thy watchers tread.
There is a rumour and a radiance of wings above my head,
An intolerable radiance of wings. . . .

All the earth grows fire,
White lips of desire
Brushing cool on the forehead, croon slumbrous things.
Earth fades; and the air is thrilled with ways,
Dewy paths full of comfort. And radiant bands,
The gracious presence of friendly hands,
Help the blind one, the glad one, who stumbles and strays,
Stretching wavering hands, up, up, through the praise
Of a myriad silver trumpets, through cries,
To all glory, to all gladness, to the infinite height,
To the gracious, the unmoving, the mother eyes,
And the laughter, and the lips, of light.

IN EXAMINATION

Lo! from quiet skies
In through the window my Lord the Sun!
And my eyes
Were dazzled and drunk with the misty gold,
The golden glory that drowned and crowned me
Eddied and swayed through the room . . .
                                        Around me,

To left and to right,
Hunched figures and old,
Dull blear-eyed scribbling fools, grew fair,
Ringed round and haloed with holy light.
Flame lit on their hair,
And their burning eyes grew young and wise,
Each as a God, or King of kings,
White-robed and bright
(Still scribbling all);
And a full tumultuous murmur of wings
Grew through the hall;
And I knew the white undying Fire,
And, through open portals,
Gyre on gyre,
Archangels and angels, adoring, bowing,
And a Face unshaded . . .
Till the light faded;
And they were but fools again, fools unknowing,
Still scribbling, blear-eyed and stolid immortals.

PINE-TREES AND THE SKY: EVENING

I'D watched the sorrow of the evening sky,
And smelt the sea, and earth, and the warm clover,
And heard the waves, and the seagull's mocking cry.

And in them all was only the old cry,
That song they always sing—"The best is over!
You may remember now, and think, and sigh,
O silly lover!"
And I was tired and sick that all was over,
And because I,
For all my thinking, never could recover
One moment of the good hours that were over.
And I was sorry and sick, and wished to die.

Then from the sad west turning wearily,
I saw the pines against the white north sky.
Very beautiful, and still, and bending over
Their sharp black heads against a quiet sky.
And there was peace in them; and I
Was happy, and forgot to play the lover,
And laughed, and did no longer wish to die;
Being glad of you, O pine-trees and the sky!

WAGNER

CREEPS in half wanton, half asleep,
One with a fat wide hairless face.
He likes love-music that is cheap;
Likes women in a crowded place;
And wants to hear the noise they're making.

His heavy eyelids droop half-over,
Great pouches swing beneath his eyes.
He listens, thinks himself the lover,
Heaves from his stomach wheezy sighs;
He likes to feel his heart's a-breaking.

The music swells. His gross legs quiver.
His little lips are bright with slime.
The music swells. The women shiver.
And all the while, in perfect time,
His pendulous stomach hangs a-shaking.

THE VISION OF THE ARCHANGELS

SLOWLY up silent peaks, the white edge of the world,
  Trod four archangels, clear against the unheeding sky,
Bearing, with quiet even steps, and great wings furled,
  A little dingy coffin; where a child must lie,
It was so tiny. (Yet, you had fancied, God could never
  Have bidden a child turn from the spring and the sunlight,
And shut him in that lonely shell, to drop for ever
  Into the emptiness and silence, into the night. . . .)

They then from the sheer summit cast, and watched it fall,
  Through unknown glooms, that frail black coffin—and
    therein
  God's little pitiful Body lying, worn and thin,
And curled up like some crumpled, lonely flower-petal—
Till it was no more visible; then turned again
With sorrowful quiet faces downward to the plain.

SEASIDE

SWIFTLY out from the friendly lilt of the band,
 The crowd's good laughter, the loved eyes of men,
 I am drawn nightward; I must turn again
Where, down beyond the low untrodden strand,
There curves and glimmers outward to the unknown
 The old unquiet ocean. All the shade
Is rife with magic and movement. I stray alone
 Here on the edge of silence, half afraid,

Waiting a sign. In the deep heart of me
The sullen waters swell towards the moon,
And all my tides set seaward.
                              From inland
Leaps a gay fragment of some mocking tune,
That tinkles and laughs and fades along the sand
And dies between the seawall and the sea.

ON THE DEATH OF SMET-SMET, THE
HIPPOPOTAMUS-GODDESS

SONG OF A TRIBE OF THE ANCIENT EGYPTIANS

(The Priests within the Temple)
SHE was wrinkled and huge and hideous? She was our Mother.
She was lustful and lewd?—but a God; we had none other.
In the day She was hidden and dumb, but at nightfall moaned
 in the shade;
We shuddered and gave Her Her will in the darkness; we
 were afraid.

(The People without)
> *She sent us pain,*
>   *And we bowed before Her;*
> *She smiled again*
>   *And bade us adore Her.*
> *She solaced our woe*
>   *And soothed our sighing;*
> *And what shall we do*
>   *Now God is dying?*

(The Priests within)
She was hungry and ate our children;—how should we stay
 Her?
She took our young men and our maidens;—ours to obey Her.
We were loathed and mocked and reviled of all nations; that
 was our pride.
She fed us, protected us, loved us, and killed us; now She has
 died.

(*The People without*)
> She was so strong;
> But death is stronger.
> She ruled us long;
> But Time is longer.
> She solaced our woe
> And soothed our sighing;
> And what shall we do
> Now God is dying?

THE SONG OF THE PILGRIMS

(Halted around the fire by night, after moon-set, they sing this beneath the trees.)

WHAT light of unremembered skies
Hast thou relumed within our eyes,
Thou whom we seek, whom we shall find? . . .
A certain odour on the wind,
Thy hidden face beyond the west,
These things have called us; on a quest
Older than any road we trod,
More endless than desire. . . .

                            Far God,

Sigh with thy cruel voice, that fills
The soul with longing for dim hills
And faint horizons! For there come
Grey moments of the antient dumb
Sickness of travel, when no song
Can cheer us; but the way seems long;
And one remembers. . . .

                          Ah! the beat

Of weary unreturning feet,
And songs of pilgrims unreturning! . . .
The fires we left are always burning
On the old shrines of home. Our kin
Have built them temples, and therein
Pray to the Gods we know; and dwell
In little houses lovable,
Being happy (we remember how!)
And peaceful even to death. . . .

                          O Thou,

God of all long desirous roaming,

Our hearts are sick of fruitless homing,
And crying after lost desire.
Hearten us onward! as with fire
Consuming dreams of other bliss.
The best Thou givest, giving this
Sufficient thing—to travel still
Over the plain, beyond the hill,
Unhesitating through the shade,
Amid the silence unafraid,
Till, at some sudden turn, one sees
Against the black and muttering trees
Thine altar, wonderfully white,
Among the Forests of the Night.

THE SONG OF THE BEASTS

(Sung, on one night, in the cities, in the darkness.)

COME away! Come away!
Ye are sober and dull through the common day,
But now it is night!
It is shameful night, and God is asleep!
(Have you not felt the quick fires that creep
Through the hungry flesh, and the lust of delight,
And hot secrets of dreams that day cannot say?)
      The house is dumb;
The night calls out to you.   Come, ah, come!
Down the dim stairs, through the creaking door,
Naked, crawling on hands and feet
—It is meet! it is meet!
Ye are men no longer, but less and more.
Beast and God. . . . Down the lampless street,
By little black ways, and secret places,
In the darkness and mire,
Faint laughter around, and evil faces
By the star-glint seen—ah! follow with us!
For the darkness whispers a blind desire,
And the fingers of night are amorous.
Keep close as we speed,
Though mad whispers woo you, and hot hands cling,
And the touch and the smell of bare flesh sting,
Soft flank by your flank, and side brushing side—
To-night never heed!
Unswerving and silent follow with me,
Till the city ends sheer,
And the crook'd lanes open wide,
Out of the voices of night,

Beyond lust and fear,
To the level waters of moonlight,
To the level waters, quiet and clear,
To the black unresting plains of the calling sea.

FAILURE

BECAUSE God put His adamantine fate
  Between my sullen heart and its desire,
I swore that I would burst the Iron Gate,
  Rise up, and curse Him on His throne of fire.
Earth shuddered at my crown of blasphemy,
  But Love was as a flame about my feet;
  Proud up the Golden Stair I strode; and beat
Thrice on the Gate, and entered with a cry—

All the great courts were quiet in the sun,
  And full of vacant echoes: moss had grown
Over the glassy pavement, and begun
  To creep within the dusty council-halls.
An idle wind blew round an empty throne
  And stirred the heavy curtains on the walls.

ANTE ARAM

BEFORE thy shrine I kneel, an unknown worshipper,
   Chanting strange hymns to thee and sorrowful litanies,
Incense of dirges, prayers that are as holy myrrh.

Ah, goddess, on thy throne of tears and faint low sighs,
   Weary at last to theeward come the feet that err,
And empty hearts grown tired of the world's vanities.

How fair this cool deep silence to a wanderer
   Deaf with the roar of winds along the open skies!
Sweet, after sting and bitter kiss of sea-water,

The pale Lethean wine within thy chalices!
   I come before thee, I, too tired wanderer,
To heed the horror of the shrine, the distant cries,

And evil whispers in the gloom, or the swift whirr
   Of terrible wings—I, least of all thy votaries,
With a faint hope to see the scented darkness stir,

And, parting, frame within its quiet mysteries
   One face, with lips than autumn-lilies tenderer,
And voice more sweet than the far plaint of viols is,

Or the soft moan of any grey-eyed lute-player.

DAWN

(From the train between Bologna and Milan, second class.)

Opposite me two Germans sweat and snore.
   Through sullen swirling gloom we jolt and roar.
We have been here for ever: even yet
   A dim watch tells two hours, two æons, more.
The windows are tight-shut and slimy-wet
   With a night's fœtor. There are two hours more;
Two hours to dawn and Milan; two hours yet.
Opposite me two Germans sweat and snore. . . .

One of them wakes, and spits, and sleeps again.
   The darkness shivers. A wan light through the rain
Strikes on our faces, drawn and white. Somewhere
   A new day sprawls; and, inside, the foul air
Is chill, and damp, and fouler than before. . . .
Opposite me two Germans sweat and snore.

THE CALL

Out of the nothingness of sleep,
   The slow dreams of Eternity,
There was a thunder on the deep:
   I came, because you called to me.

I broke the Night's primeval bars,
   I dared the old abysmal curse,
And flashed through ranks of frightened stars
   Suddenly on the universe!

The eternal silences were broken;
   Hell became Heaven as I passed.—
What shall I give you as a token,
   A sign that we have met, at last?

I'll break and forge the stars anew,
   Shatter the heavens with a song;
Immortal in my love for you,
   Because I love you, very strong.

Your mouth shall mock the old and wise,
   Your laugh shall fill the world with flame,
I'll write upon the shrinking skies
   The scarlet splendour of your name,

Till Heaven cracks, and Hell thereunder
   Dies in her ultimate mad fire,
And darkness falls, with scornful thunder,
   On dreams of men and men's desire.

[40]

Then only in the empty spaces,
　　Death, walking very silently,
Shall fear the glory of our faces
　　Through all the dark infinity.

So, clothed about with perfect love,
　　The eternal end shall find us one,
Alone above the Night, above
　　The dust of the dead gods, alone.

THE WAYFARERS

Is it the hour? We leave this resting-place
 Made fair by one another for a while.
Now, for a god-speed, one last mad embrace;
 The long road then, unlit by your faint smile.
Ah! the long road! and you so far away!
Oh, I'll remember! but . . . each crawling day
Will pale a little your scarlet lips, each mile
 Dull the dear pain of your remembered face.

. . . Do you think there's a far bordered town, somewhere,
 The desert's edge, last of the lands we know,
 Some gaunt eventual limit of our light,
 In which I'll find you waiting; and we'll go
Together, hand in hand again, out there,
 Into the waste we know not, into the night?

THE BEGINNING

SOME day I shall rise and leave my friends
And seek you again through the world's far ends,
You whom I found so fair
(Touch of your hands and smell of your hair!),
My only god in the days that were.
My eager feet shall find you again,
Though the sullen years and the mark of pain
Have changed you wholly; for I shall know
(How could I forget having loved you so?),
In the sad half-light of evening,
The face that was all my sunrising.
So then at the ends of the earth I'll stand
And hold you fiercely by either hand,
And seeing your age and ashen hair
I'll curse the thing that once you were,
Because it is changed and pale and old
(Lips that were scarlet, hair that was gold!),
And I loved you before you were old and wise,
When the flame of youth was strong in your eyes,
—And my heart is sick with memories.

1908–1911

SONNET

OH! Death will find me, long before I tire
  Of watching you; and swing me suddenly
Into the shade and loneliness and mire
  Of the last land! There, waiting patiently,

One day, I think, I'll feel a cool wind blowing,
  See a slow light across the Stygian tide,
And hear the Dead about me stir, unknowing,
  And tremble. And *I* shall know that you have died.

And watch you, a broad-browed and smiling dream,
  Pass, light as ever, through the lightless host,
Quietly ponder, start, and sway, and gleam—
  Most individual and bewildering ghost!—

And turn, and toss your brown delightful head
Amusedly, among the ancient Dead.

SONNET

I SAID I splendidly loved you; it's not true.
    Such long swift tides stir not a land-locked sea.
On gods or fools the high risk falls—on you—
    The clean clear bitter-sweet that's not for me.
Love soars from earth to ecstasies unwist.
    Love is flung Lucifer-like from Heaven to Hell.
But—there are wanderers in the middle mist,
    Who cry for shadows, clutch, and cannot tell
Whether they love at all, or, loving, whom:
    An old song's lady, a fool in fancy dress,
Or phantoms, or their own face on the gloom;
    For love of Love, or from heart's loneliness.
Pleasure's not theirs, nor pain. They doubt, and sigh,
    And do not love at all. Of these am I.

SUCCESS

I THINK if you had loved me when I wanted;
　If I'd looked up one day, and seen your eyes,
And found my wild sick blasphemous prayer granted,
　And your brown face, that's full of pity and wise,
Flushed suddenly; the white godhead in new fear
　Intolerably so struggling, and so shamed;
Most holy and far, if you'd come all too near,
　If earth had seen Earth's lordliest wild limbs tamed,
Shaken, and trapped, and shivering, for *my* touch—
　Myself should I have slain? or that foul you?
But this the strange gods, who had given so much,
　To have seen and known you, this they might not do.
One last shame's spared me, one black word's unspoken;
　And I'm alone; and you have not awoken.

DUST

When the white flame in us is gone,
   And we that lost the world's delight
Stiffen in darkness, left alone
   To crumble in our separate night;

When your swift hair is quiet in death,
   And through the lips corruption thrust
Has stilled the labour of my breath—
   When we are dust, when we are dust!—

Not dead, not undesirous yet,
   Still sentient, still unsatisfied,
We'll ride the air, and shine, and flit,
   Around the places where we died,

And dance as dust before the sun,
   And light of foot, and unconfined,
Hurry from road to road, and run
   About the errands of the wind.

And every mote, on earth or air,
   Will speed and gleam, down later days,
And like a secret pilgrim fare
   By eager and invisible ways,

Nor ever rest, nor ever lie,
   Till, beyond thinking, out of view,
One mote of all the dust that's I
   Shall meet one atom that was you.

Then in some garden hushed from wind,
  Warm in a sunset's afterglow,
The lovers in the flowers will find
  A sweet and strange unquiet grow

Upon the peace; and, past desiring,
  So high a beauty in the air,
And such a light, and such a quiring,
  And such a radiant ecstasy there,

They'll know not if it's fire, or dew,
  Or out of earth, or in the height,
Singing, or flame, or scent, or hue,
  Or two that pass, in light, to light,

Out of the garden, higher, higher. . . .
  But in that instant they shall learn
The shattering ecstasy of our fire,
  And the weak passionless hearts will burn

And faint in that amazing glow,
  Until the darkness close above;
And they will know—poor fools, they'll know!—
  One moment, what it is to love.

KINDLINESS

WHEN love has changed to kindliness—
Oh, love, our hungry lips, that press
So tight that Time's an old god's dream
Nodding in heaven, and whisper stuff
Seven million years were not enough
To think on after, make it seem
Less than the breath of children playing,
A blasphemy scarce worth the saying,
A sorry jest, "When love has grown
To kindliness—to kindliness!" . . .
And yet—the best that either's known
Will change, and wither, and be less,
At last, than comfort, or its own
Remembrance. And when some caress
Tendered in habit (once a flame
All heaven sang out to) wakes the shame
Unworded, in the steady eyes
We'll have,—*that* day, what shall we do?
Being so noble, kill the two
Who've reached their second-best? Being wise,
Break cleanly off, and get away.
Follow down other windier skies
New lures, alone? Or shall we stay,
Since this is all we've known, content
In the lean twilight of such day,
And not remember, not lament?
That time when all is over, and
Hand never flinches, brushing hand;
And blood lies quiet, for all you're near;
And it's but spoken words we hear,

Where trumpets sang; when the mere skies
Are stranger and nobler than your eyes;
And flesh is flesh, was flame before;
And infinite hungers leap no more
In the chance swaying of your dress;
And love has changed to kindliness.

MUMMIA

As those of old drank mummia
  To fire their limbs of lead,
Making dead kings from Africa
  Stand pandar to their bed;

Drunk on the dead, and medicined
  With spiced imperial dust,
In a short night they reeled to find
  Ten centuries of lust.

So I, from paint, stone, tale, and rhyme,
  Stuffed love's infinity,
And sucked all lovers of all time
  To rarify ecstasy.

Helen's the hair shuts out from me
  Verona's livid skies;
Gypsy the lips I press; and see
  Two Antonys in your eyes.

The unheard invisible lovely dead
  Lie with us in this place,
And ghostly hands above my head
  Close face to straining face;

Their blood is wine along our limbs;
  Their whispering voices wreathe
Savage forgotten drowsy hymns
  Under the names we breathe;

Woven from their tomb, and one with it,
  The night wherein we press;
Their thousand pitchy pyres have lit
  Your flaming nakedness.

For the uttermost years have cried and clung
  To kiss your mouth to mine;
And hair long dust was caught, was flung,
  Hand shaken to hand divine,

And Life has fired, and Death not shaded,
  All Time's uncounted bliss,
And the height o' the world has flamed and faded,
  Love, that our love be this!

THE FISH

In a cool curving world he lies
And ripples with dark ecstasies.
The kind luxurious lapse and steal
Shapes all his universe to feel
And know and be; the clinging stream
Closes his memory, glooms his dream,
Who lips the roots o' the shore, and glides
Superb on unreturning tides.
Those silent waters weave for him
A fluctuant mutable world and dim,
Where wavering masses bulge and gape
Mysterious, and shape to shape
Dies momently through whorl and hollow,
And form and line and solid follow
Solid and line and form to dream
Fantastic down the eternal stream;
An obscure world, a shifting world,
Bulbous, or pulled to thin, or curled,
Or serpentine, or driving arrows,
Or serene slidings, or March narrows.
There slipping wave and shore are one,
And weed and mud. No ray of sun,
But glow to glow fades down the deep
(As dream to unknown dream in sleep);
Shaken translucency illumes
The hyaline of drifting glooms;
The strange soft-handed depth subdues
Drowned colour there, but black to hues,
As death to living, decomposes—
Red darkness of the heart of roses,

Blue brilliant from dead starless skies,
And gold that lies behind the eyes,
The unknown unnameable sightless white
That is the essential flame of night,
Lustreless purple, hooded green,
The myriad hues that lie between
Darkness and darkness! . . .

                                    And all's one.

Gentle, embracing, quiet, dun,
The world he rests in, world he knows,
Perpetual curving. Only—grows
An eddy in that ordered falling,
A knowledge from the gloom, a calling
Weed in the wave, gleam in the mud—
The dark fire leaps along his blood;
Dateless and deathless, blind and still,
The intricate impulse works its will;
His woven world drops back; and he,
Sans providence, sans memory,
Unconscious and directly driven,
Fades to some dank sufficient heaven.

O world of lips, O world of laughter,
Where hope is fleet and thought flies after,
Of lights in the clear night, of cries
That drift along the wave and rise
Thin to the glittering stars above,
You know the hands, the eyes of love!
The strife of limbs, the sightless clinging,
The infinite distance, and the singing
Blown by the wind, a flame of sound,

The gleam, the flowers, and vast around
The horizon, and the heights above—
You know the sigh, the song of love!

But there the night is close, and there
Darkness is cold and strange and bare;
And the secret deeps are whisperless;
And rhythm is all deliciousness;
And joy is in the throbbing tide,
Whose intricate fingers beat and glide
In felt bewildering harmonies
Of trembling touch; and music is
The exquisite knocking of the blood.
Space is no more, under the mud;
His bliss is older than the sun.
Silent and straight the waters run.
The lights, the cries, the willows dim,
And the dark tide are one with him.

THOUGHTS ON THE SHAPE OF THE HUMAN BODY

How can we find? how can we rest? how can
We, being gods, win joy, or peace, being man?
We, the gaunt zanies of a witless Fate,
Who love the unloving and lover hate,
Forget the moment ere the moment slips,
Kiss with blind lips that seek beyond the lips,
Who want, and know not what we want, and cry
With crooked mouths for Heaven, and throw it by.
Love's for completeness! No perfection grows
'Twixt leg, and arm, elbow, and ear, and nose,
And joint, and socket; but unsatisfied
Sprawling desires, shapeless, perverse, denied.
Finger with finger wreathes; we love, and gape,
Fantastic shape to mazed fantastic shape,
Straggling, irregular, perplexed, embossed,
Grotesquely twined, extravagantly lost
By crescive paths and strange protuberant ways
From sanity and from wholeness and from grace.
How can love triumph, how can solace be,
Where fever turns toward fever, knee toward knee?
Could we but fill to harmony, and dwell
Simple as our thought and as perfectible,
Rise disentangled from humanity
Strange whole and new into simplicity,
Grow to a radiant round love, and bear
Unfluctuant passion for some perfect sphere,
Love moon to moon unquestioning, and be
Like the star Lunisequa, steadfastly
Following the round clear orb of her delight,
Patiently ever, through the eternal night!

FLIGHT

Voices out of the shade that cried,
  And long noon in the hot calm places,
And children's play by the wayside,
  And country eyes, and quiet faces—
  All these were round my steady paces.

Those that I could have loved went by me;
  Cool gardened homes slept in the sun;
I heard the whisper of water nigh me,
  Saw hands that beckoned, shone, were gone
  In the green and gold. And I went on.

For if my echoing footfall slept,
  Soon a far whispering there'd be
Of a little lonely wind that crept
  From tree to tree, and distantly
  Followed me, followed me. . . .

But the blue vaporous end of day
  Brought peace, and pursuit baffled quite,
Where between pine-woods dipped the way.
  I turned, slipped in and out of sight.
  I trod as quiet as the night.

The pine-boles kept perpetual hush;
  And in the boughs wind never swirled.
I found a flowering lowly bush,
  And bowed, slid in, and sighed and curled,
  Hidden at rest from all the world.

Safe! I was safe, and glad, I knew!
    Yet—with cold heart and cold wet brows
I lay. And the dark fell. . . . There grew
    Meward a sound of shaken boughs;
    And ceased, above my intricate house;

And silence, silence, silence found me. . . .
    I felt the unfaltering movement creep
Among the leaves. They shed around me
    Calm clouds of scent, that I did weep;
    And stroked my face. I fell asleep.

THE HILL

BREATHLESS, we flung us on the windy hill,
  Laughed in the sun, and kissed the lovely grass.
  You said, "Through glory and ecstasy we pass;
Wind, sun, and earth remain, the birds sing still,
When we are old, are old. . . ." "And when we die
  All's over that is ours; and life burns on
Through other lovers, other lips," said I,
—"Heart of my heart, our heaven is now, is won!"

"We are Earth's best, that learnt her lesson here.
  Life is our cry. We have kept the faith!" we said;
  "We shall go down with unreluctant tread
Rose-crowned into the darkness!" . . . Proud we were,
And laughed, that had such brave true things to say.
—And then you suddenly cried, and turned away.

THE ONE BEFORE THE LAST

I DREAMT I was in love again
  With the One Before the Last,
And smiled to greet the pleasant pain
  Of that innocent young past.

But I jumped to feel how sharp had been
  The pain when it did live,
How the faded dreams of Nineteen-ten
  Were Hell in Nineteen-five.

The boy's woe was as keen and clear,
  The boy's love just as true,
And the One Before the Last, my dear,
  Hurt quite as much as you.

     *   *   *   *   *

Sickly I pondered how the lover
  Wrongs the unanswering tomb,
And sentimentalizes over
  What earned a better doom.

Gently he tombs the poor dim last time,
  Strews pinkish dust above,
And sighs, "The dear dead boyish pastime!
  But *this*—ah, God!—is Love!

—Better oblivion hide dead true loves,
  Better the night enfold,
Than men, to eke the praise of new loves,
  Should lie about the old!

     *   *   *   *   *

Oh! bitter thoughts I had in plenty.
But here's the worst of it—
I shall forget, in Nineteen-twenty,
You ever hurt a bit!

THE JOLLY COMPANY

THE stars, a jolly company,
   I envied, straying late and lonely;
And cried upon their revelry:
   "O white companionship! You only
In love, in faith unbroken dwell,
Friends radiant and inseparable!"

Light-heart and glad they seemed to me
   And merry comrades (*even so*
God out of Heaven may laugh to see
   The happy crowds; and never know
That in his lone obscure distress
Each walketh in a wilderness).

But I, remembering, pitied well
   And loved them, who, with lonely light,
In empty infinite spaces dwell,
   Disconsolate. For, all the night,
I heard the thin gnat-voices cry,
Star to faint star, across the sky.

THE LIFE BEYOND

He wakes, who never thought to wake again,
    Who held the end was Death. He opens eyes
Slowly, to one long livid oozing plain
    Closed down by the strange eyeless heavens.
        He lies;
    And waits; and once in timeless sick surmise
Through the dead air heaves up an unknown hand,
Like a dry branch. No life is in that land,
    Himself not lives, but is a thing that cries;
An unmeaning point upon the mud; a speck
    Of moveless horror; an Immortal One
Cleansed of the world, sentient and dead; a fly
    Fast-stuck in grey sweat on a corpse's neck.

I thought when love for you died, I should die.
It's dead. Alone, most strangely, I live on.

LINES WRITTEN IN THE BELIEF THAT THE ANCIENT ROMAN FESTIVAL OF THE DEAD WAS CALLED AMBARVALIA

Swings the way still by hollow and hill,
    And all the world's a song;
"She's far," it sings me, "but fair," it rings me,
    "Quiet," it laughs, "and strong!"

Oh! spite of the miles and years between us,
    Spite of your chosen part,
I do remember; and I go
    With laughter in my heart.

So above the little folk that know not,
    Out of the white hill-town,
High up I clamber; and I remember;
    And watch the day go down.

Gold is my heart, and the world's golden,
    And one peak tipped with light;
And the air lies still about the hill
    With the first fear of night;

Till mystery down the soundless valley
    Thunders, and dark is here;
And the wind blows, and the light goes,
    And the night is full of fear,

And I know, one night, on some far height,
    In the tongue I never knew,

I yet shall hear the tidings clear
　From them that were friends of you.

They'll call the news from hill to hill,
　Dark and uncomforted,
Earth and sky and the winds; and I
　Shall know that you are dead.

I shall not hear your trentals,
　Nor eat your arval bread;
For the kin of you will surely do
　Their duty by the dead.

Their little dull greasy eyes will water;
　They'll paw you, and gulp afresh.
They'll sniffle and weep, and their thoughts will creep
　Like flies on the cold flesh.

They will put pence on your grey eyes,
　Bind up your fallen chin,
And lay you straight, the fools that loved you
　Because they were your kin.

They will praise all the bad about you,
　And hush the good away.
And wonder how they'll do without you,
　And then they'll go away.

But quieter than one sleeping,
　And stranger than of old,
You will not stir for weeping,
　You will not mind the cold;

But through the night the lips will laugh not,
    The hands will be in place,
And at length the hair be lying still
    About the quiet face.

With snuffle and sniff and handkerchief,
    And dim and decorous mirth,
With ham and sherry, they'll meet to bury
    The lordliest lass of earth.

The little dead hearts will tramp ungrieving
    Behind lone-riding you,
The heart so high, the heart so living,
    Heart that they never knew.

I shall not hear your trentals,
    Nor eat your arval bread,
Nor with smug breath tell lies of death
    To the unanswering dead.

With snuffle and sniff and handkerchief,
    The folk who loved you not
Will bury you, and go wondering
    Back home. And you will rot.

But laughing and half-way up to heaven,
    With wind and hill and star,
I yet shall keep, before I sleep,
    Your Ambarvalia.

DEAD MEN'S LOVE

THERE was a damned successful Poet;
   There was a Woman like the Sun.
And they were dead. They did not know it.
   They did not know their time was done.
      They did not know his hymns
      Were silence; and her limbs,
      That had served Love so well,
      Dust, and a filthy smell.

And so one day, as ever of old,
   Hands out, they hurried, knee to knee;
On fire to cling and kiss and hold
   And, in the other's eyes, to see
      Each his own tiny face,
      And in that long embrace
      Feel lip and breast grow warm
      To breast and lip and arm.

So knee to knee they sped again,
   And laugh to laugh they ran, I'm told,
Across the streets of Hell . . .
               And then,
   They suddenly felt the wind blow cold,
      And knew, so closely pressed,
      Chill air on lip and breast,
      And, with a sick surprise,
      The emptiness of eyes.

TOWN AND COUNTRY

Here, where love's stuff is body, arm and side
    Are stabbing-sweet 'gainst chair and lamp and wall.
In every touch more intimate meanings hide;
    And flaming brains are the white heart of all.

Here, million pulses to one centre beat:
    Closed in by men's vast friendliness, alone,
Two can be drunk with solitude, and meet
    On the sheer point where sense with knowing's one.

Here the green-purple clanging royal night,
    And the straight lines and silent walls of town,
And roar, and glare, and dust, and myriad white
    Undying passers, pinnacle and crown

Intensest heavens between close-lying faces
    By the lamp's airless fierce ecstatic fire;
And we've found love in little hidden places,
    Under great shades, between the mist and mire.

Stay! though the woods are quiet, and you've heard
    Night creep along the hedges. Never go
Where tangled foliage shrouds the crying bird,
    And the remote winds sigh, and waters flow!

Lest—as our words fall dumb on windless noons,
    Or hearts grow hushed and solitary, beneath
Unheeding stars and unfamiliar moons,
    Or boughs bend over, close and quiet as death,—

Unconscious and unpassionate and still,
　　Cloud-like we lean and stare as bright leaves stare,
And gradually along the stranger hill
　　Our unwalled loves thin out on vacuous air,

And suddenly there's no meaning in our kiss,
　　And your lit upward face grows, where we lie,
Lonelier and dreadfuller than sunlight is,
　　And dumb and mad and eyeless like the sky.

PARALYSIS

For moveless limbs no pity I crave,
   That never were swift! Still all I prize,
Laughter and thought and friends, I have;
   No fool to heave luxurious sighs
For the woods and hills that I never knew.
The more excellent way's yet mine! And you

Flower-laden come to the clean white cell,
   And we talk as ever—am I not the same?
With our hearts we love, immutable,
   You without pity, I without shame.
We talk as of old; as of old you go
Out under the sky, and laughing, I know,

Flit through the streets, your heart all me;
   Till you gain the world beyond the town.
Then—I fade from your heart, quietly;
   And your fleet steps quicken. The strong down
Smiles you welcome there; the woods that love you
Close lovely and conquering arms above you.

O ever-moving, O lithe and free!
   Fast in my linen prison I press
On impassable bars, or emptily
   Laugh in my great loneliness.
And still in the white neat bed I strive
Most impotently against that gyve;
Being less now than a thought, even,
To you alone with your hills and heaven.

MENELAUS AND HELEN

I

Hor through Troy's ruin Menelaus broke
　To Priam's palace, sword in hand, to sate
　On that adulterous whore a ten years' hate
And a king's honour. Through red death, and smoke,
And cries, and then by quieter ways he strode,
　　Till the still innermost chamber fronted him.
　He swung his sword, and crashed into the dim
Luxurious bower, flaming like a god.

High sat white Helen, lonely and serene.
　He had not remembered that she was so fair,
And that her neck curved down in such a way;
And he felt tired. He flung the sword away,
　And kissed her feet, and knelt before her there,
The perfect Knight before the perfect Queen.

II

So far the poet. How should he behold
　That journey home, the long connubial years?
　He does not tell you how white Helen bears
Child on legitimate child, becomes a scold,
Haggard with virtue. Menelaus bold
　Waxed garrulous, and sacked a hundred Troys
　'Twixt noon and supper. And her golden voice
Got shrill as he grew deafer. And both were old.

Often he wonders why on earth he went
　Troyward, or why poor Paris ever came.
Oft she weeps, gummy-eyed and impotent;
　Her dry shanks twist at Paris' mumbled name.
So Menelaus nagged; and Helen cried;
And Paris slept on by Scamander side.

LIBIDO

How should I know? The enormous wheels of will
  Drove me cold-eyed on tired and sleepless feet.
Night was void arms and you a phantom still,
  And day your far light swaying down the street.
As never fool for love, I starved for you;
  My throat was dry and my eyes hot to see.
Your mouth so lying was most heaven in view,
  And your remembered smell most agony.

Love wakens love! I felt your hot wrist shiver
  And suddenly the mad victory I planned
    Flashed real, in your burning bending head. . . .
My conqueror's blood was cool as a deep river
  In shadow; and my heart beneath your hand
    Quieter than a dead man on a bed.

JEALOUSY

When I see you, who were so wise and cool,
Gazing with silly sickness on that fool
You've given your love to, your adoring hands
Touch his so intimately that each understands,
I know, most hidden things; and when I know
Your holiest dreams yield to the stupid bow
Of his red lips, and that the empty grace
Of those strong legs and arms, that rosy face,
Has beaten your heart to such a flame of love,
That you have given him every touch and move,
Wrinkle and secret of you, all your life,
—Oh! then I know I'm waiting, lover-wife,
For the great time when love is at a close,
And all its fruit's to watch the thickening nose
And sweaty neck and dulling face and eye,
That are yours, and you, most surely, till you die!
Day after day you'll sit with him and note
The greasier tie, the dingy wrinkling coat;
As prettiness turns to pomp, and strength to fat,
And love, love, love to habit!

                        And after that,
When all that's fine in man is at an end,
And you, that loved young life and clean, must tend
A foul sick fumbling dribbling body and old,
When his rare lips hang flabby and can't hold
Slobber, and you're enduring that worst thing,
Senility's queasy furtive love-making,
And searching those dear eyes for human meaning,
Propping the bald and helpless head, and cleaning

A scrap that life's flung by, and love's forgotten,—
Then you'll be tired; and passion dead and rotten;
And he'll be dirty, dirty!

                        O lithe and free
And lightfoot, that the poor heart cries to see,
That's how I'll see your man and you!—

                              But you
—Oh, when *that* time comes, you'll be dirty too!

BLUE EVENING

My restless blood now lies a-quiver,
  Knowing that always, exquisitely,
This April twilight on the river
  Stirs anguish in the heart of me.

For the fast world in that rare glimmer
  Puts on the witchery of a dream,
The straight grey buildings, richly dimmer,
  The fiery windows, and the stream

With willows leaning quietly over,
  The still ecstatic fading skies . . .
And all these, like a waiting lover,
  Murmur and gleam, lift lustrous eyes,

Drift close to me, and sideways bending
  Whisper delicious words.
                                        But I
Stretch terrible hands, uncomprehending,
  Shaken with love; and laugh; and cry.

My agony made the willows quiver;
  I heard the knocking of my heart
Die loudly down the windless river,
  I heard the pale skies fall apart,

And the shrill stars' unmeaning laughter,
  And my voice with the vocal trees
Weeping. And Hatred followed after,
  Shrilling madly down the breeze.

[78]

In peace from the wild heart of clamour,
  A flower in moonlight, she was there,
Was rippling down white ways of glamour
  Quietly laid on wave and air.

Her passing left no leaf a-quiver.
  Pale flowers wreathed her white, white brows.
Her feet were silence on the river;
  And "Hush!" she said, between the boughs.

THE CHARM

In darkness the loud sea makes moan;
And earth is shaken, and all evils creep
About her ways.
                      Oh, now to know you sleep!
Out of the whirling blinding moil, alone,
Out of the slow grim fight,
One thought to wing—to you, asleep,
In some cool room that's open to the night
Lying half-forward, breathing quietly,
One white hand on the white
Unrumpled sheet, and the ever-moving hair
Quiet and still at length! . . .

Your magic and your beauty and your strength,
Like hills at noon or sunlight on a tree,
Sleeping prevail in earth and air.

In the sweet gloom above the brown and white
Night benedictions hover; and the winds of night
Move gently round the room, and watch you there.
And through the dreadful hours
The trees and waters and the hills have kept
The sacred vigil while you slept,
And lay a way of dew and flowers
Where your feet, your morning feet, shall tread.

And still the darkness ebbs about your bed.
Quiet, and strange, and loving-kind, you sleep.
And holy joy about the earth is shed;
And holiness upon the deep.

FINDING

F<small>ROM</small> the candles and dumb shadows,
  And the house where love had died,
I stole to the vast moonlight
  And the whispering life outside.
But I found no lips of comfort,
  No home in the moon's light
(I, little and lone and frightened
  In the unfriendly night),
And no meaning in the voices. . . .
  Far over the lands and through
The dark, beyond the ocean,
  I willed to think of *you!*
For I knew, had you been with me
  I'd have known the words of night,
Found peace of heart, gone gladly
  In comfort of that light.

Oh! the wind with soft beguiling
  Would have stolen my thought away;
And the night, subtly smiling,
  Came by the silver way;
And the moon came down and danced to me,
  And her robe was white and flying;
And trees bent their heads to me
  Mysteriously crying;
And dead voices wept around me;
  And dead soft fingers thrilled;
And the little gods whispered. . . .
                 But ever

    Desperately I willed;

Till all grew soft and far
　　And silent . . .
　　　　　　　　　And suddenly
I found you white and radiant,
　　Sleeping quietly,
Far out through the tides of darkness.
　　And I there in that great light
Was alone no more, nor fearful;
　　For there, in the homely night,
Was no thought else that mattered,
　　And nothing else was true,
But the white fire of moonlight,
　　And a white dream of you.

SONG

"Oh! Love," they said, "is King of Kings,
  And Triumph is his crown.
Earth fades in flame before his wings,
  And Sun and Moon bow down."—
But that, I knew, would never do;
  And Heaven is all too high.
So whenever I met a Queen, I said,
  I will not catch her eye.

"Oh! Love," they said, and "Love," they said,
  "The gift of Love is this;
A crown of thorns about thy head,
  And vinegar to thy kiss!"—
But Tragedy is not for me;
  And I'm content to be gay.
So whenever I spied a Tragic Lady,
  I went another way.

And so I never feared to see
  You wander down the street,
Or come across the fields to me
  On ordinary feet.
For what they'd never told me of,
  And what I never knew;
It was that all the time, my love,
  Love would be merely you.

THE VOICE

SAFE in the magic of my woods
   I lay, and watched the dying light.
Faint in the pale high solitudes,
   And washed with rain and veiled by night,

Silver and blue and green were showing.
   And the dark woods grew darker still;
And birds were hushed; and peace was growing;
   And quietness crept up the hill;

   And no wind was blowing

And I knew
That this was the hour of knowing,
And the night and the woods and you
Were one together, and I should find
Soon in the silence the hidden key
Of all that had hurt and puzzled me—
Why you were you, and the night was kind,
And the woods were part of the heart of me.

And there I waited breathlessly,
Alone; and slowly the holy three,
The three that I loved, together grew
One, in the hour of knowing,
Night, and the woods, and you—
And suddenly
There was an uproar in my woods,

The noise of a fool in mock distress,
Crashing and laughing and blindly going,
Of ignorant feet and a swishing dress,
And a Voice profaning the solitudes.

The spell was broken, the key denied me
And at length your flat clear voice beside me
Mouthed cheerful clear flat platitudes.

You came and quacked beside me in the wood.
You said, "The view from here is very good!"
You said, "It's nice to be alone a bit!"
And, "How the days are drawing out!" you said.
You said, "The sunset's pretty, isn't it?"

   * * * * *

By God! I wish—I wish that you were dead!

DINING-ROOM TEA

WHEN you were there, and you, and you,
Happiness crowned the night; I too,
Laughing and looking, one of all,
I watched the quivering lamplight fall
On plate and flowers and pouring tea
And cup and cloth; and they and we
Flung all the dancing moments by
With jest and glitter. Lip and eye
Flashed on the glory, shone and cried,
Improvident, unmemoried;
And fitfully and like a flame
The light of laughter went and came.
Proud in their careless transience moved
The changing faces that I loved.

Till suddenly, and otherwhence,
I looked upon your innocence.
For lifted clear and still and strange
From the dark woven flow of change
Under a vast and starless sky
I saw the immortal moment lie.
One instant I, an instant, knew
As God knows all. And it and you
I, above Time, oh, blind! could see
In witless immortality.

I saw the marble cup; the tea,
Hung on the air, an amber stream;
I saw the fire's unglittering gleam,
The painted flame, the frozen smoke.

No more the flooding lamplight broke
On flying eyes and lips and hair;
But lay, but slept unbroken there,
On stiller flesh, and body breathless,
And lips and laughter stayed and deathless,
And words on which no silence grew.
Light was more alive than you.

For suddenly, and otherwhence,
I looked on your magnificence.
I saw the stillness and the light,
And you, august, immortal, white,
Holy and strange; and every glint
Posture and jest and thought and tint
Freed from the mask of transiency,
Triumphant in eternity,
Immote, immortal.

                           Dazed at length
Human eyes grew, mortal strength
Wearied; and Time began to creep.
Change closed about me like a sleep.
Light glinted on the eyes I loved.
The cup was filled. The bodies moved.
The drifting petal came to ground.
The laughter chimed its perfect round.
The broken syllable was ended.
And I, so certain and so friended,
How could I cloud, or how distress,
The heaven of your unconsciousness?
Or shake at Time's sufficient spell,
Stammering of lights unutterable?

The eternal holiness of you,
The timeless end, you never knew,
The peace that lay, the light that shone.
You never knew that I had gone
A million miles away, and stayed
A million years. The laughter played
Unbroken round me; and the jest
Flashed on. And we that knew the best
Down wonderful hours grew happier yet.
I sang at heart, and talked, and ate,
And lived from laugh to laugh, I too,
When you were there, and you, and you.

THE GODDESS IN THE WOOD

In a flowered dell the Lady Venus stood,
  Amazed with sorrow. Down the morning one
  Far golden horn in the gold of trees and sun
Rang out; and held; and died. . . . She thought the wood
Grew quieter. Wing, and leaf, and pool of light
  Forgot to dance. Dumb lay the unfalling stream;
  Life one eternal instant rose in dream
Clear out of time, poised on a golden height. . . .

Till a swift terror broke the abrupt hour.
The gold waves purled amidst the green above her;
  And a bird sang. With one sharp-taken breath,
By sunlit branches and unshaken flower,
The immortal limbs flashed to the human lover,
  And the immortal eyes to look on death.

A CHANNEL PASSAGE

THE damned ship lurched and slithered. Quiet and quick
  My cold gorge rose; the long sea rolled; I knew
I must think hard of something, or be sick;
  And could think hard of only one thing—*you!*
You, you alone could hold my fancy ever!
  And with you memories come, sharp pain, and dole.
Now there's a choice—heartache or tortured liver!
  A sea-sick body, or a you-sick soul!

Do I forget you? Retchings twist and tie me,
  Old meat, good meals, brown gobbets, up I throw.
Do I remember? Acrid return and slimy,
  The sobs and slobber of a last year's woe.
And still the sick ship rolls. 'Tis hard, I tell ye,
To choose 'twixt love and nausea, heart and belly.

VICTORY

ALL night the ways of Heaven were desolate,
   Long roads across a gleaming empty sky.
   Outcast and doomed and driven, you and I,
Alone, serene beyond all love or hate,
Terror or triumph, were content to wait,
   We, silent and all-knowing. Suddenly
   Swept through the heaven low-crouching from on high,
One horseman, downward to the earth's low gate.
Oh, perfect from the ultimate height of living,
   Lightly we turned, through wet woods blossom-hung,
Into the open. Down the supernal roads,
   With plumes a-tossing, purple flags far flung,
Rank upon rank, unbridled, unforgiving,
   Thundered the black battalions of the Gods.

DAY AND NIGHT

THROUGH my heart's palace Thoughts unnumbered throng;
 And there, most quiet and, as a child, most wise,
High-throned you sit, and gracious. All day long
 Great Hopes gold-armoured, jester Fantasies,
 And pilgrim Dreams, and little beggar Sighs,
Bow to your benediction, go their way.
 And the grave jewelled courtier Memories
Worship and love and tend you, all the day.

But when I sleep, and all my thoughts go straying,
 When the high session of the day is ended,
And darkness comes; then, with the waning light,
 By lilied maidens on your way attended,
Proud from the wonted throne, superbly swaying,
 You, like a queen, pass out into the night.

Experiments

CHORIAMBICS—I.

Ah! not now, when desire burns, and the wind calls, and the
    suns of spring
Light-foot dance in the woods, whisper of life, woo me to
    wayfaring;
Ah! not now should you come, now when the road beckons,
    and good friends call,
Where are songs to be sung, fights to be fought, yea! and the
    best of all,
Love, on myriad lips fairer than yours, kisses you could not
    give! . . .
Dearest, why should I mourn, whimper, and whine, I that
    have yet to live?
Sorrow will I forget, tears for the best, love on the lips of you,
Now, when dawn in the blood wakes, and the sun laughs up
    the eastern blue;
I'll forget and be glad!
    Only at length, dear, when the great day ends,
When love dies with the last light, and the last song has been
    sung, and friends
All are perished, and gloom strides on the heaven: then, as
    alone I lie,
'Mid Death's gathering winds, frightened and dumb, sick for
    the past, may I
Feel you suddenly there, cool at my brow; then may I hear
    the peace
Of your voice at the last, whispering love, calling, ere all can
    cease
In the silence of death; then may I see dimly, and know, a
    space,
Bending over me, last light in the dark, once, as of old, your
    face.

CHORIAMBICS—II.

Here the flame that was ash, shrine that was void, lost in the
haunted wood,
I have tended and loved, year upon year, I in the solitude
Waiting, quiet and glad-eyed in the dark, knowing that once
a gleam
Glowed and went through the wood. Still I abode strong in
a golden dream,
Unrecaptured.
　　　　　For I, I that had faith, knew that a face would
　　　　　　　glance
One day, white in the dim woods, and a voice call, and a
radiance
Fill the grove, and the fire suddenly leap . . . and, in the
heart of it,
End of labouring, you! Therefore I kept ready the altar, lit
The flame, burning apart.
　　　　　Face of my dreams vainly in vision white
Gleaming down to me, lo! hopeless I rise now. For about mid-
night
Whispers grew through the wood suddenly, strange cries in
the boughs above
Grated, cries like a laugh. Silent and black then through the
sacred grove
Great birds flew, as a dream, troubling the leaves, passing at
length.
　　　　　I knew
Long expected and long loved, that afar, God of the dim wood,
you
Somewhere lay, as a child sleeping, a child suddenly reft from
mirth,

[96]

White and wonderful yet, white in your youth, stretched upon
    foreign earth,
God, immortal and dead!
      Therefore I go; never to rest, or win
Peace, and worship of you more, and the dumb wood and
    the shrine therein.

DESERTION

So light we were, so right we were, so fair faith shone,
And the way was laid so certainly, that, when I'd gone,
What dumb thing looked up at you? Was it something heard,
Or a sudden cry, that meekly and without a word
You broke the faith, and strangely, weakly, slipped apart?
You gave in—you, the proud of heart, unbowed of heart!
Was this, friend, the end of all that we could do?
And have you found the best for you, the rest for you?
Did you learn so suddenly (and I not by!)
Some whispered story, that stole the glory from the sky,
And ended all the splendid dream, and made you go
So dully from the fight we know, the light we know?

O faithless! the faith remains, and I must pass
Gay down the way, and on alone. Under the grass
You wait; the breeze moves in the trees, and stirs, and calls,
And covers you with white petals, with light petals.
There it shall crumble, frail and fair, under the sun,
O little heart, your brittle heart; till day be done,
And the shadows gather, falling light, and, white with dew,
Whisper, and weep; and creep to you. Good sleep to you!

1914

I. PEACE

Now, God be thanked Who has matched us with His hour,
  And caught our youth, and wakened us from sleeping,
With hand made sure, clear eye, and sharpened power,
  To turn, as swimmers into cleanness leaping,
Glad from a world grown old and cold and weary,
  Leave the sick hearts that honour could not move,
And half-men, and their dirty songs and dreary,
  And all the little emptiness of love!

Oh! we, who have known shame, we have found release there,
  Where there's no ill, no grief, but sleep has mending,
    Naught broken save this body, lost but breath;
Nothing to shake the laughing heart's long peace there
  But only agony, and that has ending;
    And the worst friend and enemy is but Death.

II. SAFETY

Dear! of all happy in the hour, most blest
   He who has found our hid security,
Assured in the dark tides of the world that rest,
   And heard our word, "Who is so safe as we?"
We have found safety with all things undying,
   The winds, and morning, tears of men and mirth,
The deep night, and birds singing, and clouds flying,
   And sleep, and freedom, and the autumnal earth.
We have built a house that is not for Time's throwing.
   We have gained a peace unshaken by pain for ever.
War knows no power. Safe shall be my going,
   Secretly armed against all death's endeavour;
Safe though all safety's lost; safe where men fall;
And if these poor limbs die, safest of all.

III. THE DEAD

Blow out, you bugles, over the rich Dead!
    There's none of these so lonely and poor of old,
    But, dying, has made us rarer gifts than gold.
These laid the world away; poured out the red
Sweet wine of youth; gave up the years to be
    Of work and joy, and that unhoped serene,
    That men call age; and those who would have been,
Their sons, they gave, their immortality.

Blow, bugles, blow! They brought us, for our dearth,
    Holiness, lacked so long, and Love, and Pain.
Honour has come back, as a king, to earth,
    And paid his subjects with a royal wage;
And Nobleness walks in our ways again;
    And we have come into our heritage.

IV. THE DEAD

These hearts were woven of human joys and cares,
  Washed marvellously with sorrow, swift to mirth.
The years had given them kindness. Dawn was theirs,
  And sunset, and the colours of the earth.
These had seen movement, and heard music; known
  Slumber and waking; loved; gone proudly friended;
Felt the quick stir of wonder; sat alone;
  Touched flowers and furs and cheeks. All this is ended.

There are waters blown by changing winds to laughter
And lit by the rich skies, all day. And after,
  Frost, with a gesture, stays the waves that dance
And wandering loveliness. He leaves a white
  Unbroken glory, a gathered radiance,
A width, a shining peace, under the night.

V. THE SOLDIER

If I should die, think only this of me:
   That there's some corner of a foreign field
That is for ever England. There shall be
   In that rich earth a richer dust concealed;
A dust whom England bore, shaped, made aware,
   Gave, once, her flowers to love, her ways to roam,
A body of England's, breathing English air,
   Washed by the rivers, blest by suns of home.

And think, this heart, all evil shed away,
   A pulse in the eternal mind, no less
      Gives somewhere back the thoughts by England given;
Her sights and sounds; dreams happy as her day;
   And laughter, learnt of friends; and gentleness,
      In hearts at peace, under an English heaven.

THE TREASURE

WHEN colour goes home into the eyes,
    And lights that shine are shut again
With dancing girls and sweet birds' cries
    Behind the gateways of the brain;
And that no-place which gave them birth, shall close
The rainbow and the rose:—

Still may Time hold some golden space
    Where I'll unpack that scented store
Of song and flower and sky and face,
    And count, and touch, and turn them o'er,
Musing upon them; as a mother, who
Has watched her children all the rich day through
Sits, quiet-handed, in the fading light,
When children sleep, ere night.

The South Seas

TIARE TAHI'TI

MAMUA, when our laughter ends,
And hearts and bodies, brown as white,
Are dust about the doors of friends,
Or scent ablowing down the night,
Then, oh! then, the wise agree,
Comes our immortality.
Mamua, there waits a land
Hard for us to understand.
Out of time, beyond the sun,
All are one in Paradise,
You and Pupure are one,
And Taü, and the ungainly wise.
There the Eternals are, and there
The Good, the Lovely, and the True,
And Types, whose earthly copies were
The foolish broken things we knew;
There is the Face, whose ghosts we are;
The real, the never-setting Star;
And the Flower, of which we love
Faint and fading shadows here;
Never a tear, but only Grief;
Dance, but not the limbs that move;
Songs in Song shall disappear;
Instead of lovers, Love shall be;
For hearts, Immutability;
And there, on the Ideal Reef,
Thunders the Everlasting Sea!

And my laughter, and my pain,
Shall home to the Eternal Brain.

And all lovely things, they say,
Meet in Loveliness again;
Miri's laugh, Teïpo's feet,
And the hands of Matua,
Stars and sunlight there shall meet,
Coral's hues and rainbows there,
And Teüra's braided hair;
And with the starred *tiare's* white,
And white birds in the dark ravine,
And *flamboyants* ablaze at night,
And jewels, and evening's after-green,
And dawns of pearl and gold and red,
Mamua, your lovelier head!
And there'll no more be one who dreams
Under the ferns, of crumbling stuff,
Eyes of illusion, mouth that seems,
All time-entangled human love.
And you'll no longer swing and sway
Divinely down the scented shade,
Where feet to Ambulation fade,
And moons are lost in endless Day.
How shall we wind these wreaths of ours,
Where there are neither heads nor flowers?
Oh, Heaven's Heaven!—but we'll be missing
The palms, and sunlight, and the south;
And there's an end, I think, of kissing,
When our mouths are one with Mouth. . . .

    Taü here, Mamua,
Crown the hair, and come away!
Hear the calling of the moon,
And the whispering scents that stray

About the idle warm lagoon.
Hasten, hand in human hand,
Down the dark, the flowered way,
Along the whiteness of the sand,
And in the water's soft caress,
Wash the mind of foolishness,
Mamua, until the day.
Spend the glittering moonlight there
Pursuing down the soundless deep
Limbs that gleam and shadowy hair,
Or floating lazy, half-asleep.
Dive and double and follow after,
Snare in flowers, and kiss, and call,
With lips that fade, and human laughter
And faces individual,
Well this side of Paradise! . . .
There's little comfort in the wise.

PAPEETE, *February*, 1914

RETROSPECT

In your arms was still delight,
Quiet as a street at night;
And thoughts of you, I do remember,
Were green leaves in a darkened chamber,
Were dark clouds in a moonless sky.
Love, in you, went passing by,
Penetrative, remote, and rare,
Like a bird in the wide air,
And, as the bird, it left no trace
In the heaven of your face.
In your stupidity I found
The sweet hush after a sweet sound.
All about you was the light
That dims the greying end of night;
Desire was the unrisen sun,
Joy the day not yet begun,
With tree whispering to tree,
Without wind, quietly.
Wisdom slept within your hair,
And Long-Suffering was there,
And, in the flowing of your dress,
Undiscerning Tenderness.
And when you thought, it seemed to me,
Infinitely, and like a sea,
About the slight world you had known
Your vast unconsciousness was thrown. . . .

O haven without wave or tide!
Silence, in which all songs have died!
Holy book, where hearts are still!

And home at length under the hill!
O mother quiet, breasts of peace,
Where love itself would faint and cease!
O infinite deep I never knew,
I would come back, come back to you,
Find you, as a pool unstirred,
Kneel down by you, and never a word,
Lay my head, and nothing said,
In your hands, ungarlanded;
And a long watch you would keep;
And I should sleep, and I should sleep!

MATAIEA, *January*, 1914

THE GREAT LOVER

I HAVE been so great a lover: filled my days
So proudly with the splendour of Love's praise,
The pain, the calm, and the astonishment,
Desire illimitable, and still content,
And all dear names men use, to cheat despair,
For the perplexed and viewless streams that bear
Our hearts at random down the dark of life.
Now, ere the unthinking silence on that strife
Steals down, I would cheat drowsy Death so far,
My night shall be remembered for a star
That outshone all the suns of all men's days.
Shall I not crown them with immortal praise
Whom I have loved, who have given me, dared with me
High secrets, and in darkness knelt to see
The inenarrable godhead of delight?
Love is a flame;—we have beaconed the world's night.
A city:—and we have built it, these and I.
An emperor:—we have taught the world to die.
So, for their sakes I loved, ere I go hence,
And the high cause of Love's magnificence,
And to keep loyalties young, I'll write those names
Golden for ever, eagles, crying flames,
And set them as a banner, that men may know,
To dare the generations, burn, and blow
Out on the wind of Time, shining and streaming. . . .

These I have loved:
                White plates and cups, clean-gleaming,
Ringed with blue lines; and feathery, faëry dust;
Wet roofs, beneath the lamp-light; the strong crust

Of friendly bread; and many-tasting food;
Rainbows; and the blue bitter smoke of wood;
And radiant raindrops couching in cool flowers;
And flowers themselves, that sway through sunny hours,
Dreaming of moths that drink them under the moon;
Then, the cool kindliness of sheets, that soon
Smooth away trouble; and the rough male kiss
Of blankets; grainy wood; live hair that is
Shining and free; blue-massing clouds; the keen
Unpassioned beauty of a great machine;
The benison of hot water; furs to touch;
The good smell of old clothes; and other such—
The comfortable smell of friendly fingers,
Hair's fragrance, and the musty reek that lingers
About dead leaves and last year's ferns. . . .

                                        Dear names,
And thousand other throng to me! Royal flames;
Sweet water's dimpling laugh from tap or spring;
Holes in the ground; and voices that do sing;
Voices in laughter, too; and body's pain,
Soon turned to peace; and the deep-panting train;
Firm sands; the little dulling edge of foam
That browns and dwindles as the wave goes home;
And washen stones, gay for an hour; the cold
Graveness of iron; moist black earthen mould;
Sleep; and high places; footprints in the dew;
And oaks; and brown horse-chestnuts, glossy-new;
And new-peeled sticks; and shining pools on grass;—
All these have been my loves. And these shall pass,
Whatever passes not, in the great hour,
Nor all my passion, all my prayers, have power
To hold them with me through the gate of Death.

They'll play deserter, turn with the traitor breath,
Break the high bond we made, and sell Love's trust
And sacramented covenant to the dust.
—Oh, never a doubt but, somewhere, I shall wake,
And give what's left of love again, and make
New friends, now strangers. . . .

                But the best I've known,
Stays here, and changes, breaks, grows old, is blown
About the winds of the world, and fades from brains
Of living men, and dies.

                   Nothing remains.

O dear my loves, O faithless, once again
This one last gift I give: that after men
Shall know, and later lovers, far-removed,
Praise you, "All these were lovely"; say, "He loved."

MATAIEA, 1914

HEAVEN

Fish (fly-replete, in depth of June,
Dawdling away their wat'ry noon)
Ponder deep wisdom, dark or clear,
Each secret fishy hope or fear.
Fish say, they have their Stream and Pond;
But is there anything Beyond?
This life cannot be All, they swear,
For how unpleasant, if it were!
One may not doubt that, somehow, Good
Shall come of Water and of Mud;
And, sure, the reverent eye must see
A Purpose in Liquidity.
We darkly know, by Faith we cry,
The future is not Wholly Dry.
Mud unto mud!—Death eddies near—
Not here the appointed End, not here!
But somewhere, beyond Space and Time.
Is wetter water, slimier slime!
And there (they trust) there swimmeth One
Who swam ere rivers were begun,
Immense, of fishy form and mind,
Squamous, omnipotent, and kind;
And under that Almighty Fin,
The littlest fish may enter in.
Oh! never fly conceals a hook,
Fish say, in the Eternal Brook,
But more than mundane weeds are there,
And mud, celestially fair;
Fat caterpillars drift around,
And Paradisal grubs are found;

Unfading moths, immortal flies,
And the worm that never dies.
And in that Heaven of all their wish,
There shall be no more land, say fish.

DOUBTS

When she sleeps, her soul, I know,
Goes a wanderer on the air,
Wings where I may never go,
Leaves her lying, still and fair,
Waiting, empty, laid aside,
Like a dress upon a chair. . . .
This I know, and yet I know
Doubts that will not be denied.

For if the soul be not in place,
What has laid trouble in her face?
And, sits there nothing ware and wise
Behind the curtains of her eyes,
What is it, in the self's eclipse,
Shadows, soft and passingly,
About the corners of her lips,
The smile that is essential she?

And if the spirit be not there,
Why is fragrance in the hair?

THERE'S WISDOM IN WOMEN

"Oh love is fair, and love is rare"; my dear one she said,
"But love goes lightly over." I bowed her foolish head,
And kissed her hair and laughed at her. Such a child was she;
So new to love, so true to love, and she spoke so bitterly.

But there's wisdom in women, of more than they have known,
And thoughts go blowing through them, are wiser than their
    own,
Or how should my dear one, being ignorant and young,
Have cried on love so bitterly, with so true a tongue?

HE WONDERS WHETHER TO PRAISE OR
TO BLAME HER

I HAVE peace to weigh your worth, now all is over,
    But if to praise or blame you, cannot say.
For, who decries the loved, decries the lover;
    Yet what man lauds the thing he's thrown away?

Be you, in truth, this dull, slight, cloudy naught,
    The more fool I, so great a fool to adore;
But if you're that high goddess once I thought,
    The more your godhead is, I lose the more.

Dear fool, pity the fool who thought you clever!
    Dear wisdom, do not mock the fool that missed you!
Most fair,—the blind has lost your face for ever!
    Most foul,—how could I see you while I kissed you?

So . . . the poor love of fools and blind I've proved you,
For, foul or lovely, 'twas a fool that loved you.

A MEMORY (From a sonnet-sequence)

SOMEWHILE before the dawn I rose, and stept
  Softly along the dim way to your room,
  And found you sleeping in the quiet gloom,
And holiness about you as you slept.
I knelt there; till your waking fingers crept
  About my head, and held it. I had rest
  Unhoped this side of Heaven, beneath your breast.
I knelt a long time, still; nor even wept.

It was great wrong you did me; and for gain
Of that poor moment's kindliness, and ease,
And sleepy mother-comfort!
                Child, you know
How easily love leaps out to dreams like these,
Who has seen them true. And love that's wakened so
Takes all too long to lay asleep again.

WAIKIKI, *October*, 1913

ONE DAY

TODAY I have been happy. All the day
   I held the memory of you, and wove
Its laughter with the dancing light o' the spray,
   And sowed the sky with tiny clouds of love,
And sent you following the white waves of sea,
   And crowned your head with fancies, nothing worth,
Stray buds from that old dust of misery,
   Being glad with a new foolish quiet mirth.

So lightly I played with those dark memories,
Just as a child, beneath the summer skies,
   Plays hour by hour with a strange shining stone,
For which (he knows not) towns were fire of old,
   And love has been betrayed, and murder done,
And great kings turned to a little bitter mould.

THE PACIFIC, *October*, 1913

WAIKIKI

Warm perfumes like a breath from vine and tree
   Drift down the darkness. Plangent, hidden from eyes
   Somewhere an *eukaleli* thrills and cries
And stabs with pain the night's brown savagery.
And dark scents whisper; and dim waves creep to me,
   Gleam like a woman's hair, stretch out, and rise;
   And new stars burn into the ancient skies,
Over the murmurous soft Hawaiian sea.

And I recall, lose, grasp, forget again,
   And still remember, a tale I have heard, or known,
An empty tale, of idleness and pain,
   Of two that loved—or did not love—and one
Whose perplexed heart did evil, foolishly,
A long while since, and by some other sea.

Waikiki, 1913

HAUNTINGS

In the grey tumult of these after years
  Oft silence falls; the incessant wranglers part;
And less-than-echoes of remembered tears
  Hush all the loud confusion of the heart;
And a shade, through the toss'd ranks of mirth and crying
  Hungers, and pains, and each dull passionate mood,—
Quite lost, and all but all forgot, undying,
  Comes back the ecstasy of your quietude.

So a poor ghost, beside his misty streams,
Is haunted by strange doubts, evasive dreams,
  Hints of a pre-Lethean life, of men,
Stars, rocks, and flesh, things unintelligible,
  And light on waving grass, he knows not when,
And feet that ran, but where, he cannot tell.

THE PACIFIC, 1914

SONNET (Suggested by some of the Proceedings of the Society for Psychical Research)

Not with vain tears, when we're beyond the sun,
    We'll beat on the substantial doors, nor tread
    Those dusty high-roads of the aimless dead
Plaintive for Earth; but rather turn and run
Down some close-covered by-way of the air,
    Some low sweet alley between wind and wind,
    Stoop under faint gleams, thread the shadows, find
Some whispering ghost-forgotten nook, and there

Spend in pure converse our eternal day;
    Think each in each, immediately wise;
Learn all we lacked before; hear, know, and say
    What this tumultuous body now denies;
And feel, who have laid our groping hands away;
    And see, no longer blinded by our eyes.

CLOUDS

Down the blue night the unending columns press
   In noiseless tumult, break and wave and flow,
   Now tread the far South, or lift rounds of snow
Up to the white moon's hidden loveliness.
Some pause in their grave wandering comradeless,
   And turn with profound gesture vague and slow,
   As who would pray good for the world, but know
Their benediction empty as they bless.

They say that the Dead die not, but remain
   Near to the rich heirs of their grief and mirth.
     I think they ride the calm mid-heaven, as these,
In wise majestic melancholy train,
     And watch the moon, and the still-raging seas,
     And men, coming and going on the earth.

THE PACIFIC, *October*, 1913

MUTABILITY

THEY say there's a high windless world and strange,
  Out of the wash of days and temporal tide,
  Where Faith and Good, Wisdom and Truth abide,
Æterna corpora, subject to no change.
There the sure suns of these pale shadows move;
  There stand the immortal ensigns of our war;
  Our melting flesh fixed Beauty there, a star,
And perishing hearts, imperishable Love. . . .

Dear, we know only that we sigh, kiss, smile;
  Each kiss lasts but the kissing; and grief goes over;
  Love has no habitation but the heart.
Poor straws! on the dark flood we catch awhile,
  Cling, and are borne into the night apart.
  The laugh dies with the lips, "Love" with the lover.

SOUTH KENSINGTON—MAKAWELI, 1913

Other Poems

THE BUSY HEART

Now that we've done our best and worst, and parted,
  I would fill my mind with thoughts that will not rend.
(O heart, I do not dare go empty-hearted)
  I'll think of Love in books, Love without end;
Women with child, content; and old men sleeping;
  And wet strong ploughlands, scarred for certain grain;
And babes that weep, and so forget their weeping;
  And the young heavens, forgetful after rain;
And evening hush, broken by homing wings;
  And Song's nobility, and Wisdom holy,
That live, we dead. I would think of a thousand things,
  Lovely and durable, and taste them slowly,
One after one, like tasting a sweet food.
I have need to busy my heart with quietude.

LOVE

Love is a breach in the walls, a broken gate,
　　Where that comes in that shall not go again;
Love sells the proud heart's citadel to Fate.
　　They have known shame, who love unloved. Even then,
When two mouths, thirsty each for each, find slaking,
　　And agony's forgot, and hushed the crying
Of credulous hearts, in heaven—such are but taking
　　Their own poor dreams within their arms, and lying
Each in his lonely night, each with a ghost.
　　Some share that night. But they know love grows colder,
Grows false and dull, that was sweet lies at most.
　　Astonishment is no more in hand or shoulder,
But darkens, and dies out from kiss to kiss.
All this is love; and all love is but this.

UNFORTUNATE

HEART, you are restless as a paper scrap
  That's tossed down dusty pavements by the wind;
  Saying, "She is most wise, patient and kind.
Between the small hands folded in her lap
Surely a shamed head may bow down at length,
  And find forgiveness where the shadows stir
About her lips, and wisdom in her strength,
  Peace in her peace. Come to her, come to her!" . . .

She will not care. She'll smile to see me come,
  So that I think all Heaven in flower to fold me.
  She'll give me all I ask, kiss me and hold me,
    And open wide upon that holy air
The gates of peace, and take my tiredness home,
  Kinder than God. But, heart, she will not care.

THE CHILTERNS

Your hands, my dear, adorable,
  Your lips of tenderness
—Oh, I've loved you faithfully and well,
  Three years, or a bit less.
  It wasn't a success.

Thank God, that's done! and I'll take the road,
  Quit of my youth and you,
The Roman road to Wendover
  By Tring and Lilley Hoo,
  As a free man may do.

For youth goes over, the joys that fly,
  The tears that follow fast;
And the dirtiest things we do must lie
  Forgotten at the last;
  Even Love goes past.

What's left behind I shall not find,
  The splendour and the pain;
The splash of sun, the shouting wind,
  And the brave sting of rain,
  I may not meet again.

But the years, that take the best away,
  Give something in the end;
And a better friend than love have they,
  For none to mar or mend,
  That have themselves to friend.

I shall desire and I shall find
  The best of my desires;
The autumn road, the mellow wind
  That soothes the darkening shires.
  And laughter, and inn-fires.

White mist about the black hedgerows,
  The slumbering Midland plain,
The silence where the clover grows,
  And the dead leaves in the lane,
  Certainly, these remain.

And I shall find some girl perhaps,
  And a better one than you,
With eyes as wise, but kindlier,
  And lips as soft, but true.
  And I daresay she will do.

HOME

I CAME back late and tired last night
  Into my little room,
To the long chair and the firelight
  And comfortable gloom.

But as I entered softly in
  I saw a woman there,
The line of neck and cheek and chin,
  The darkness of her hair,
The form of one I did not know
  Sitting in my chair.

I stood a moment fierce and still,
  Watching her neck and hair.
I made a step to her; and saw
  That there was no one there.

It was some trick of the firelight
  That made me see her there.
It was a chance of shade and light
  And the cushion in the chair.

Oh, all you happy over the earth,
  That night, how could I sleep?
I lay and watched the lonely gloom;
  And watched the moonlight creep
From wall to basin, round the room.
  All night I could not sleep.

THE NIGHT JOURNEY

HANDS and lit faces eddy to a line;
   The dazed last minutes click; the clamour dies.
Beyond the great-swung arc o' the roof, divine,
   Night, smoky-scarv'd, with thousand coloured eyes

Glares the imperious mystery of the way.
   Thirsty for dark, you feel the long-limbed train
Throb, stretch, thrill motion, slide, pull out and sway,
   Strain for the far, pause, draw to strength again. . . .

As a man, caught by some great hour, will rise,
   Slow-limbed, to meet the light or find his love;
And, breathing long, with staring sightless eyes,
   Hands out, head back, agape and silent, move

Sure as a flood, smooth as a vast wind blowing;
   And, gathering power and purpose as he goes,
Unstumbling, unreluctant, strong, unknowing,
   Borne by a will not his, that lifts, that grows,

Sweep out to darkness, triumphing in his goal,
   Out of the fire, out of the little room. . . .
—There is an end appointed, O my soul!
   Crimson and green the signals burn; the gloom

Is hung with steam's far-blowing livid streamers.
   Lost into God, as lights in light, we fly,
Grown one with will, end-drunken huddled dreamers.
   The white lights roar. The sounds of the world die.

And lips and laughter are forgotten things.
  Speed sharpens; grows. Into the night, and on,
The strength and splendour of our purpose swings.
  The lamps fade; and the stars. We are alone.

SONG

ALL suddenly the wind comes soft,
   And Spring is here again;
And the hawthorn quickens with buds of green,
   And my heart with buds of pain.

My heart all Winter lay so numb,
   The earth so dead and frore,
That I never thought the Spring would come,
   Or my heart wake any more.

But Winter's broken and earth has woken,
   And the small birds cry again;
And the hawthorn hedge puts forth its buds,
   And my heart puts forth its pain.

BEAUTY AND BEAUTY

WHEN Beauty and Beauty meet
   All naked, fair to fair,
The earth is crying-sweet,
   And scattering-bright the air,
Eddying, dizzying, closing round,
   With soft and drunken laughter;
Veiling all that may befall
   After—after—

Where Beauty and Beauty met,
   Earth's still a-tremble there,
And winds are scented yet,
   And memory-soft the air,
Bosoming, folding glints of light,
   And shreds of shadowy laughter;
Not the tears that fill the years
   After—after—

THE WAY THAT LOVERS USE

THE way that lovers use is this;
  They bow, catch hands, with never a word,
And their lips meet, and they do kiss,
  —So I have heard.

They queerly find some healing so,
  And strange attainment in the touch;
There is a secret lovers know,
  —I have read as much.

And theirs no longer joy nor smart,
  Changing or ending, night or day;
But mouth to mouth, and heart on heart,
  —So lovers say.

MARY AND GABRIEL

Young Mary, loitering once her garden way,
Felt a warm splendour grow in the April day,
As wine that blushes water through. And soon,
Out of the gold air of the afternoon,
One knelt before her: hair he had, or fire,
Bound back above his ears with golden wire,
Baring the eager marble of his face.
Not man's or woman's was the immortal grace
Rounding the limbs beneath that robe of white,
And lighting the proud eyes with changeless light,
Incurious. Calm as his wings, and fair,
That presence filled the garden.

                           She stood there,
Saying, "What would you, Sir?"

                              He told his word,
"Blessed art thou of women!" Half she heard,
Hands folded and face bowed, half long had known,
The message of that clear and holy tone,
That fluttered hot sweet sobs about her heart;
Such serene tidings moved such human smart.
Her breath came quick as little flakes of snow.
Her hands crept up her breast. She did but know
It was not hers. She felt a trembling stir
Within her body, a will too strong for her
That held and filled and mastered all. With eyes
Closed, and a thousand soft short broken sighs,
She gave submission; fearful, meek, and glad. . . .

She wished to speak. Under her breasts she had
Such multitudinous burnings, to and fro,
And throbs not understood; she did not know

If they were hurt or joy for her; but only
That she was grown strange to herself, half lonely,
All wonderful, filled full of pains to come
And thoughts she dare not think, swift thoughts and dumb,
Human, and quaint, her own, yet very far,
Divine, dear, terrible, familiar . . .
Her heart was faint for telling; to relate
Her limbs' sweet treachery, her strange high estate,
Over and over, whispering, half revealing,
Weeping; and so find kindness to her healing.
'Twixt tears and laughter, panic hurrying her,
She raised her eyes to that fair messenger.
He knelt unmoved, immortal; with his eyes
Gazing beyond her, calm to the calm skies;
Radiant, untroubled in his wisdom, kind.
His sheaf of lilies stirred not in the wind.
How should she, pitiful with mortality,
Try the wide peace of that felicity
With ripples of her perplexed shaken heart,
And hints of human ecstasy, human smart,
And whispers of the lonely weight she bore,
And how her womb within was hers no more
And at length hers?
           Being tired, she bowed her head;
And said, "So be it!"
              The great wings were spread
Showering glory on the fields, and fire.
The whole air, singing, bore him up, and higher,
Unswerving, unreluctant. Soon he shone
A gold speck in the gold skies; then was gone.

The air was colder, and grey. She stood alone.

THE FUNERAL OF YOUTH: THRENODY

THE day that *Youth* had died,
There came to his grave-side,
In decent mourning, from the country's end,
Those scatter'd friends
Who had lived the boon companions of his prime,
And laughed with him and sung with him and wasted,
In feast and wine and many-crown'd carouse,
The days and nights and dawnings of the time
When *Youth* kept open house,
Nor left untasted
Aught of his high emprise and ventures dear,
No quest of his unshar'd—
All these, with loitering feet and sad head bar'd,
Followed their old friend's bier.
Folly went first,
With muffled bells and coxcomb still revers'd;
And after trod the bearers, hat in hand—
Laughter, most hoarse, and Captain *Pride* with tanned
And martial face all grim, and fussy *Joy*,
Who had to catch a train, and *Lust*, poor, snivelling boy;
These bore the dear departed.
Behind them, broken-hearted,
Came *Grief*, so noisy a widow, that all said,
"Had he but wed
Her elder sister *Sorrow*, in her stead!"
And by her, trying to soothe her all the time,
The fatherless children, *Colour*, *Tune*, and *Rhyme*
(The sweet lad *Rhyme*), ran all-uncomprehending.
Then, at the way's sad ending,
Round the raw grave they stay'd. Old *Wisdom* read, ...

[144]

In mumbling tone, the Service for the Dead.
There stood *Romance*,
The furrowing tears had mark'd her rougèd cheek;
Poor old *Conceit*, his wonder unassuaged;
Dead *Innocency's* daughter, *Ignorance*;
And shabby, ill-dress'd *Generosity*;
And *Argument*, too full of woe to speak;
Passion, grown portly, something middle-aged;
And *Friendship*—not a minute older, she;
Impatience, ever taking out his watch;
Faith, who was deaf, and had to lean, to catch
Old *Wisdom's* endless drone.
Beauty was there,
Pale in her black; dry-eyed; she stood alone.
Poor maz'd *Imagination*; *Fancy* wild;
Ardour, the sunlight on his greying hair;
Contentment, who had known *Youth* as a child
And never seen him since. And *Spring* came too,
Dancing over the tombs, and brought him flowers—
She did not stay for long.
And *Truth*, and *Grace*, and all the merry crew,
The laughing *Winds* and *Rivers*, and lithe *Hours*;
And *Hope*, the dewy-eyed; and sorrowing *Song*;—
Yes, with much woe and mourning general,
At dead *Youth's* funeral,
Even these were met once more together, all,
Who erst the fair and living *Youth* did know;
All, except only *Love*. *Love* had died long ago.

Grantchester

THE OLD VICARAGE, GRANTCHESTER

(Café des Westens, Berlin, May, 1912)

JUST now the lilac is in bloom,
All before my little room;
And in my flower-beds, I think,
Smile the carnation and the pink;
And down the borders, well I know,
The poppy and the pansy blow . . .
Oh! there the chestnuts, summer through,
Beside the river make for you
A tunnel of green gloom, and sleep
Deeply above; and green and deep
The stream mysterious glides beneath,
Green as a dream and deep as death.
—Oh, damn! I know it! and I know
How the May fields all golden show,
And when the day is young and sweet,
Gild gloriously the bare feet
That run to bathe . . .
                              Du lieber Gott!

Here am I, sweating, sick, and hot,
And there the shadowed waters fresh
Lean up to embrace the naked flesh.
Temperamentvoll German Jews
Drink beer around;—and *there* the dews
Are soft beneath a morn of gold.
Here tulips bloom as they are told;
Unkempt about those hedges blows
An English unofficial rose;
And there the unregulated sun

Slopes down to rest when day is done,
And wakes a vague unpunctual star,
A slippered Hesper; and there are
Meads towards Haslingfield and Coton
Where *das Betreten's* not *verboten*.

εἴθε γενοίμην . . . would I were
In Grantchester, in Grantchester!—
Some, it may be, can get in touch
With Nature there, or Earth, or such.
And clever modern men have seen
A Faun a-peeping through the green,
And felt the Classics were not dead,
To glimpse a Naiad's reedy head,
Or hear the Goat-foot piping low: . . .
But these are things I do not know.
I only know that you may lie
Day long and watch the Cambridge sky,
And, flower-lulled in sleepy grass,
Hear the cool lapse of hours pass,
Until the centuries blend and blur
In Grantchester, in Grantchester. . . .
Still in the dawnlit waters cool
His ghostly Lordship swims his pool,
And tries the strokes, essays the tricks,
Long learnt on Hellespont, or Styx.
Dan Chaucer hears his river still
Chatter beneath a phantom mill.
Tennyson notes, with studious eye,
How Cambridge waters hurry by . . .
And in that garden, black and white,
Creep whispers through the grass all night;

And spectral dance, before the dawn,
A hundred Vicars down the lawn;
Curates, long dust, will come and go
On lissom, clerical, printless toe;
And oft between the boughs is seen
The sly shade of a Rural Dean . . .
Till, at a shiver in the skies,
Vanishing the Satanic cries,
The prim ecclesiastic rout
Leaves but a startled sleeper-out,
Grey heavens, the first bird's drowsy calls,
The falling house that never falls.

God! I will pack, and take a train,
And get me to England once again!
For England's the one land, I know,
Where men with Splendid Hearts may go;
And Cambridgeshire, of all England,
The shire for Men who Understand;
And of *that* district I prefer
The lovely hamlet Grantchester.
For Cambridge people rarely smile,
Being urban, squat, and packed with guile;
And Royston men in the far South
Are black and fierce and strange of mouth;
At Over they fling oaths at one,
And worse than oaths at Trumpington,

And Ditton girls are mean and dirty,
And there's none in Harston under thirty,
And folks in Shelford and those parts
Have twisted lips and twisted hearts,

And Barton men make Cockney rhymes,
And Coton's full of nameless crimes,
And things are done you'd not believe
At Madingley on Christmas Eve.
Strong men have run for miles and miles,
When one from Cherry Hinton smiles;
Strong men have blanched, and shot their wives,
Rather than send them to St. Ives;
Strong men have cried like babes, bydam,
To hear what happened at Babraham.
But Grantchester! ah, Grantchester!
There's peace and holy quiet there,
Great clouds along pacific skies,
And men and women with straight eyes,
Lithe children lovelier than a dream,
A bosky wood, a slumbrous stream,
And little kindly winds that creep
Round twilight corners, half asleep.
In Grantchester their skins are white;
They bathe by day, they bathe by night;
The women there do all they ought;
The men observe the Rules of Thought.
They love the Good; they worship Truth;
They laugh uproariously in youth;
(And when they get to feeling old,
They up and shoot themselves, I'm told) . . .

Ah God! to see the branches stir
Across the moon at Grantchester!
To smell the thrilling-sweet and rotten
Unforgettable, unforgotten
River-smell, and hear the breeze

Sobbing in the little trees.
Say, do the elm-clumps greatly stand
Still guardians of that holy land?
The chestnuts shade, in reverend dream,
The yet unacademic stream?
Is dawn a secret shy and cold
Anadyomene, silver-gold?
And sunset still a golden sea
From Haslingfield to Madingley?
And after, ere the night is born,
Do hares come out about the corn?
Oh, is the water sweet and cool,
Gentle and brown, above the pool?
And laughs the immortal river still
Under the mill, under the mill?
Say, is there Beauty yet to find?
And Certainty? and Quiet kind?
Deep meadows yet, for to forget
The lies, and truths, and pain? . . . oh! yet
Stands the Church clock at ten to three?
And is there honey still for tea?

FAFAÏA

Stars that seem so close and bright,
Watched by lovers through the night,
Swim in emptiness, men say,
Many a mile and year away.

And yonder star that burns so white,
May have died to dust and night
Ten, maybe, or fifteen year,
Before it shines upon my dear.

Oh! often among men below,
Heart cries out to heart, I know,
And one is dust a many years,
Child, before the other hears.

Heart from heart is all as far,
Fafaïa, as star from star.

Saanapu, *November,* 1913.

Appendix

NOTE

The Appendix contains: (1) the only two coherent fragments found in the notebook which Brooke used in the last month of his life; a little song, written, I think on his travels; and a poem, dating probably from 1912, which for some reason he left unrevised; (2) a few "lighter" poems which I dare say he would have printed on their merits if he had published a volume in which they would not have been out of key. Two of these, the "Letter to a Live Poet" and "The Little Dog's Day," were written for *Westminster Gazette* competitions, in which they won prizes.

EDWARD MARSH

FRAGMENT

I STRAYED about the deck, an hour, to-night
Under a cloudy moonless sky; and peeped
In at the windows, watched my friends at table,
Or playing cards, or standing in the doorway,
Or coming out into the darkness. Still
No one could see me.

                 I would have thought of them
—Heedless, within a week of battle—in pity,
Pride in their strength and in the weight and firmness
And link'd beauty of bodies, and pity that
This gay machine of splendour 'ld soon be broken,
Thought little of, pashed, scattered. . . .

                   Only, always,
I could but see them—against the lamplight—pass
Like coloured shadows, thinner than filmy glass,
Slight bubbles, fainter than the wave's faint light,
That broke to phosphorus out in the night,
Perishing things and strange ghosts—soon to die
To other ghosts—this one, or that, or I.

April, 1915.

THE DANCE

A Song

As the Wind, and as the Wind,
　　In a corner of the way,
Goes stepping, stands twirling,
Invisibly, comes whirling,
Bows before, and skips behind,
　　In a grave, an endless play—

So my Heart, and so my Heart,
　　Following where your feet have gone,
Stirs dust of old dreams there;
He turns a toe; he gleams there,
Treading you a dance apart.
　　But you see not. You pass on.

April, 1915.

SONG

THE way of love was thus.
He was born one winter morn
With hands delicious,
And it was well with us.

Love came our quiet way,
Lit pride in us, and died in us,
All in a winter's day.
There is no more to say.

1913 (?).

SOMETIMES EVEN NOW . . .

SOMETIMES even now I may
Steal a prisoner's holiday,
Slip, when all is worst, the bands,
  Hurry back, and duck beneath
Time's old tyrannous groping hands,
  Speed away with laughing breath
Back to all I'll never know,
Back to you, a year ago.

Truant there from Time and Pain,
What I had, I find again:
Sunlight in the boughs above,
  Sunlight in your hair and dress,
The Hands too proud for all but Love,
  The Lips of utter kindliness,
The Heart of bravery swift and clean
  Where the best was safe, I knew,
And laughter in the gold and green,
  And song, and friends, and ever you
With smiling and familiar eyes,
  You—but friendly: you—but true.

And Innocence accounted wise,
  And Faith the fool, the pitiable.
Love so rare, one would swear
  All of earth for ever well—
Careless lips and flying hair,
  And little things I may not tell.

It does but double the heart-ache
When I wake, when I wake.

1912 (?).

SONNET: IN TIME OF REVOLT

THE Thing must End. I am no boy! I AM
   No BOY! ! being twenty-one. Uncle, you make
   A great mistake, a very great mistake,
In chiding me for letting slip a "Damn!"
What's more, you called me "Mother's one ewe lamb,"
   Bade me "refrain from swearing—for *her* sake—
   Till I'm grown up" . . . —By God! I think you take
Too much upon you, Uncle William!

You say I am your brother's only son.
I know it. And, "What of it?" I reply.
My heart's resolvèd. *Something must be done.*
So shall I curb, so baffle, so suppress
This too avuncular officiousness,
Intolerable consanguinity.

January, 1908.

A LETTER TO A LIVE POET

Sir, since the last Elizabethan died,
Or, rather, that more Paradisal muse,
Blind with much light, passed to the light more glorious
Or deeper blindness, no man's hand, as thine,
Has, on the world's most noblest chord of song,
Struck certain magic strains. Ears satiate
With the clamorous, timorous whisperings of to-day,
Thrilled to perceive once more the spacious voice
And serene utterance of old. We heard
—With rapturous breath half-held, as a dreamer dreams
Who dares not know it dreaming, lest he wake—
The odorous, amorous style of poetry,
The melancholy knocking of those lines,
The long, low soughing of pentameters,
—Or the sharp of rhyme as a bird's cry—
And the innumerable truant polysyllables
Multitudinously twittering like a bee.
Fulfilled our hearts were with that music then,
And all the evenings sighed it to the dawn,
And all the lovers heard it from all the trees.
All of the accents upon all the norms!
—And ah! the stress on the penultimate!
We never knew blank verse could have such feet.

Where is it now? Oh, more than ever, now
I sometimes think no poetry is read
Save where some sepultured Cæsura bled,
Royally incarnadining all the line.
Is the imperial iamb laid to rest,
And the young trochee, having done enough?

Ah! turn again! Sing so to us, who are sick
Of seeming-simple rhymes, bizarre emotions,
Decked in the simple verses of the day,
Infinite meaning in a little gloom,
Irregular thoughts in stanzas regular,
Modern despair in antique metres, myths
Incomprehensible at evening,
And symbols that mean nothing in the dawn.
The slow lines swell. The new style sighs. The Celt
Moans round with many voices.

                    God! to see
Gaunt anapæsts stand up out of the verse,
Combative accents, stress where no stress should be.
Spondee on spondee, iamb on choriamb,
The thrill of all the tribrachs in the world,
And all the vowels rising to the E!
To hear the blessed mutter of those verbs,
Conjunctions passionate toward each other's arms,
And epithets like amaranthine lovers
Stretching luxuriously to the stars,
All prouder pronouns than the dawn, and all
The thunder of the trumpets of the noun!

January, 1911.

FRAGMENT ON PAINTERS

THERE is an evil which that Race attaints
Who represent God's World with oily paints,
Who mock the Universe, so rare and sweet,
With spots of colour on a canvas sheet,
Defile the Lovely and insult the Good
By scrawling upon little bits of wood.
They'd snare the moon, and catch the immortal sun
With madder brown and pale vermilion,
Entrap an English evening's magic hush . . .

.   .   .   .

THE TRUE BEATITUDE (Bouts-Rimés)

THEY say, when the Great Prompter's hand shall ring
　　Down the last curtain upon earth and sea,
　　All the Good Mimes will have eternity
To praise their Author, worship love and sing;
Or to the walls of Heaven wandering
　　Look down on those damned for a fretful d——,
　　Mock them (all theologians agree
On this reward for virtue), laugh, and fling

New sulphur on the sin-incarnadined . . .
　　Ah, Love! still temporal, and still atmospheric,
　　Teleologically unperturbed,
We share a peace by no divine divined,
　　An earthly garden hidden from any cleric,
　　Untrodden of God, by no Eternal curbed.

1913.

SONNET REVERSED

Hand trembling towards hand; the amazing lights
Of heart and eye. They stood on supreme heights.

Ah, the delirious weeks of honeymoon!
   Soon they returned, and, after strange adventures,
Settled at Balham by the end of June.
   Their money was in Can. Pacs. B. Debentures,
And in Antofagastas. Still he went
   Cityward daily; still she did abide
At home. And both were really quite content
   With work and social pleasures. Then they died.
They left three children (besides George, who drank):
   The eldest Jane, who married Mr. Bell,
William, the head-clerk in the County Bank,
   And Henry, a stock-broker, doing well.

LULWORTH, 1 *January*, 1911.

IT'S NOT GOING TO HAPPEN AGAIN

I HAVE known the most dear that is granted us here,
   More supreme than the gods know above,
Like a star I was hurled through the sweet of the world,
   And the height and the light of it, Love.
I have risen to the uttermost Heaven of Joy,
   I have sunk to the sheer Hell of Pain—
But—it's not going to happen again, my boy,
   It's not going to happen again.

It's the very first word that poor Juliet heard
   From her Romeo over the Styx;
And the Roman will tell Cleopatra in hell
   When she starts her immortal old tricks;
What Paris was tellin' for good-bye to Helen
   When he bundled her into the train—
Oh, it's not going to happen again, old girl,
   It's not going to happen again.

CHATEAU LAKE LOUISE, CANADA, 1913.

THE LITTLE DOG'S DAY

All in the town were still asleep,
When the sun came up with a shout and a leap.
In the lonely streets unseen by man,
A little dog danced. And the day began.

ALL his life he'd been good, as far as he could,
And the poor little beast had done all that he should.
But this morning he swore, by Odin and Thor
And the Canine Valhalla—he'd stand it no more!

So his prayer he got granted—to do just what he wanted,
Prevented by none, for the space of one day.
"Jam incipiebo,[1] *sedere facebo,"* [2]
In dog-Latin he quoth, *"Euge! sophos! hurray!"*

He fought with the he-dogs, and winked at the she-dogs,
A thing that had never been *heard* of before.
"For the stigma of gluttony, I care not a button!" he
Cried, and ate all he could swallow—and more.

He took sinewy lumps from the shins of old frumps,
And mangled the errand-boys—when he could get 'em.
He shammed furious *rabies,*[3] and bit all the babies,[3]
And followed the cats up the trees, and then ate 'em!

They thought 'twas the devil was holding a revel,
And sent for the parson to drive him away;
For the town never knew such a hullabaloo
As that little dog raised—till the end of that day.

[1] Now we're off.   [2] *I'll* make them sit up.
[3] Pronounce either to suit rhyme.

When the blood-red sun had gone burning down,
And the lights were lit in the little town,
Outside, in the gloom of the twilight grey,
The little dog died when he'd had his day.

July, 1907.

RUPERT BROOKE

A BIOGRAPHICAL NOTE

ANY biographical account of Rupert Brooke must of necessity be brief; yet it is well to know the facts of his romantic career, and to see him as far as may be through the eyes of those who knew him (the writer was unfortunately not of this number) in order the better to appreciate his work.

He was born at Rugby on August 3, 1887, his father, William Brooke, being an assistant master at the school. Here Brooke was educated, and in 1905 won a prize for a poem called "The Bastille," which has been described as "fine, fluent stuff." He took a keen interest in every form of athletic sport, and played both cricket and football for the school. Though he afterwards dropped both these games, he developed as a sound tennis player, was a great walker, and found joy in swimming, like Byron and Swinburne, especially by night. He delighted in the Russian ballet and went again and again to a good Revue.

In 1906 he went up to King's College, Cambridge, where he made innumerable friends, and was considered one of the leading intellectuals of his day, among his peers being James Elroy Flecker, himself a poet of no small achievement, who died at Davos only a few months ago. Mr. Ivan Lake, the editor of the *Bodleian*, a contemporary at Cambridge, tells me that although the two men moved in different sets, they frequented the same literary circles. Brooke, however, seldom, if ever, spoke at the Union, but was a member of the Cambridge Fabian Society, and held the posts of Secretary and President in turn. His socialism was accompanied by a passing phase of vegetarianism, and with the ferment of youth working headily within him he could hardly escape the charge of being a crank, but "a crank, if a little thing, makes revolutions," and Brooke's youthful extravagances were utterly untinged with decadence. He took his classical tripos in 1909, and after spending some time as a student in Munich, returned to live near Cambridge at the Old Vicarage in "the lovely hamlet, Grantchester." "It was there," writes Mr. Raglan H. E. H. Somerset in a letter I am privileged to quote, "that I used to wake him on Sunday mornings to bathe in the dam above Byron's Pool. His bedroom was always littered with books, English, French, and German, in wild disorder. About his bathing one thing stands out; time after time he would try to dive; he always failed and came absolutely flat, but seemed to like it, although it must have hurt excessively." (This was only when he was learning. Later he became an accomplished diver.) "Then we used to go back and feed, sometimes in the Orchard and sometimes in the Old Vicarage Garden, on eggs and that particular brand of honey referred to in the 'Grantchester' poem. In those days he always dressed in the same way: cricket shirt and trousers and no stockings; in fact, 'Rupert's mobile toes' were a subject for the admiration of his friends."

Brooke occupied himself mainly with writing. Poems, remarkable for a happy spontaneity such as characterized the work of T. E. Brown, the Manx poet, appeared in the *Gownsman*, the *Cambridge Review*, the *Nation*, the *English Review*, and the *Westminster Gazette*. Students of the "Problem Page" in the *Saturday Westminster* knew him as a brilliant competitor who infused the purely academic with the very spirit of youth.

To all who knew him, the man himself was at least as important as his work. "As to his talk"—I quote again from Mr. Somerset—"he was a spendthrift. I mean that he never saved anything up as those writer fellows so often do. He was quite inconsequent and just rippled on, but was always ready to attack a careless thinker. On the other hand, he was extremely tolerant of fools, even bad poets who are the worst kind of fools—or rather the hardest to bear—but that was kindness of heart."

Of his personal appearance a good deal has been said. "One who knew him," writing in one of the daily papers, said that "to look at, he was part of the youth of the world. He was one of the handsomest Englishmen of his time. His moods seemed to be merely a disguise for the radiance of an early summer's day."

Mr. Edward Thomas speaks of him as "a golden young Apollo" who made friends, admirers, adorers, wherever he went. "He stretched himself out, drew his fingers through his waved fair hair, laughed, talked indolently, and admired as much as he was admired. . . . He was tall, broad, and easy in his movements. Either he stooped, or he thrust his head forward unusually much to look at you with his steady blue eyes."

On Mr. H. W. Nevinson, who, in a fleeting editorial capacity, sent for Brooke to come and discuss his poems, he made a similar impression:

"Suddenly he came—an astonishing apparition in any newspaper office: loose hair of deep, browny-gold; smooth, ruddy face; eyes not grey or bluish-white, but of living blue, really like the sky, and as frankly open; figure not very tall, but firm and strongly made, giving the sense of weight rather than of speed and yet so finely fashioned and healthy that it was impossible not to think of the line about 'a pard-like spirit.' He was dressed just in the ordinary way, except that he wore a low blue collar, and blue shirt and tie, all uncommon in those days. Evidently he did not want to be conspicuous, but the whole effect was almost ludicrously beautiful."

Notions of height are always comparative, and it will be noticed that Mr. Nevinson and Mr. Thomas differ in their ideas. Mr. Edward Marsh, however, Brooke's executor and one of his closest friends—indeed the friend of all young poets —tells me that he was about six feet, so that all doubt on this minor point may be set at rest.

He had been in Munich, Berlin, and in Italy, and in May, 1913, he left England again for a wander year, passing through the United States and Canada on his way to the South Seas. Perhaps some of those who met him in Boston and elsewhere will some day contribute their quota to the bright record of his life. His own letters to the *Westminster Gazette*, though naturally of unequal merit, were full of humorous delight in the New World. In one of his travel papers he described the city of Quebec as having "the radiance and repose of an immortal." "That, in so many words," wrote Mr. Walter de la Mare, "brings back his living remembrance. . . . With him there was a happy shining impression that he might have just come—that very moment—from another planet, one well within the solar system, but a little more like Utopia than ours." Not even Stevenson, it would seem, excited a greater enthusiasm among his friends; and between the two men an interesting parallel might be drawn. Brooke made a pilgrimage to Stevenson's home in Samoa, and his life in the Pacific found full and happy expression in his verse. His thoughts, however, turned longingly to England, the land "where Men with Splendid Hearts may go," and he reappeared from the ends of the earth among his friends as apparently little changed "as one who gaily and laughingly goes to bed and gaily and laughingly comes down next morning after a perfectly refreshing sleep."

Then came the War. "Well, if Armageddon's *on*," he said, "I suppose one should be there." It was a characteristic way of putting it. He obtained a commission in the Hood Battalion of the Royal Naval Division in September, and was quickly ordered on the disastrous if heroic expedition to Antwerp. Here he had his first experience of war, lying for some days in trenches shelled by the distant German guns. Then followed a strange retreat by night along roads lit by the glare of burning towns, and swarming with pitiful crowds of Belgian refugees. Yet as Mr. Walter de la Mare said of him, when he returned from Antwerp, "Ulysses himself at the end of his voyagings was not more quietly accustomed to the shocks of novelty."

On Brooke, as on many other young men, to whom the gift of self-expression has perhaps been denied, the war had a swiftly maturing influence. Much of the impetuosity of youth fell away from him. The boy who had been rather proud of his independent views—a friend relates how at the age of twelve he sat on the platform at a pro-Boer meeting—grew suddenly, it seemed, into a man filled with the love of life indeed, but inspired most of all with the love of England. Fortunately for himself and for us, Brooke's patriotism found passionate voice in the sonnets which are rightly given pride of place in the 1914 section of this volume. Mr. Clement Shorter, who gives us the skeleton of a bibliography that is all too brief, draws special attention to *New Numbers*, a quarterly publication issued in Gloucestershire, to which Brooke contributed in February, April, August, and December of last year, his fellow poets being Lascelles Abercrombie, John Drinkwater, and Wilfrid Wilson Gibson. He spent the winter in training at Blandford Camp in Dorsetshire, and sailed with the British Mediterranean Expeditionary Force on the last day of Febru-

[174]

ary. He had a presentiment of his death, but he went, as so
many others have gone,

> "Unstumbling, unreluctant, strong, unknowing,
>   Borne by a will not his, that lifts, that grows,
> Sweeps out to darkness, triumphing in his goal,
>   Out of the fire, out of the little room. . . .
> —There is an end appointed, O my soul!"—

He never reached the Dardanelles. He went first to Lemnos
and then to Egypt. Early in April he had a touch of sunstroke
from which he recovered; but he died from blood-poisoning
on board a French hospital ship at Scyros on Friday, April
23rd—died for England on the day of St. Michael and St.
George. He was buried at night, by torchlight, in an olive
grove about a mile inland. "If you go there," writes Mr.
Stephen Graham, "you will find a little wooden cross with
just his name and the date of his birth and his death marked
on it in black." A few days later the news of his death was published in the *Times* with the following appreciation:

"W. S. C." writes: "Rupert Brooke is dead. A telegram
from the Admiral at Lemnos tells us that this life has closed
at the moment when it seemed to have reached its spring-
time. A voice had become audible, a note had been struck,
more true, more thrilling, more able to do justice to the nobility of our youth in arms engaged in this present war, than any
other—more able to express their thoughts of self-surrender,
and with a power to carry comfort to those who watch them
so intently from afar. The voice has been swiftly stilled. Only
the echoes and the memory remain; but they will linger.

"During the last few months of his life, months of prepara-
tion in gallant comradeship and open air, the poet-soldier told
with all the simple force of genius the sorrow of youth about

to die, and the sure, triumphant consolations of a sincere and valiant spirit. He expected to die; he was willing to die for the dear England whose beauty and majesty he knew; and he advanced toward the brink in perfect serenity, with absolute conviction of the rightness of his country's cause and a heart devoid of hate for fellowmen.

"The thoughts to which he gave expression in the very few incomparable war sonnets which he has left behind will be shared by many thousands of young men moving resolutely and blithely forward into this, the hardest, the cruelest, and the least-rewarded of all the wars that men have fought. They are a whole history and revelation of Rupert Brooke himself. Joyous, fearless, versatile, deeply instructed, with classic symmetry of mind and body, ruled by high, undoubting purpose, he was all that one would wish England's noblest sons to be in days when no sacrifice but the most precious is acceptable, and the most precious is that which is most freely proffered."

"W. S. C.," as many probably guessed at the time, was the Rt. Hon. Winston Spencer Churchill, a personal friend and warm admirer of the poet. Many other tributes followed, notably from an anonymous writer in the *Spectator*, from Mr. Walter de la Mare, Mr. Edward Thomas, Mr. Holbrook Jackson, Mr. Jack Collings Squire, Mr. James Douglas, Mr. Drinkwater, Mr. Gibson, and Mr. Lascelles Abercrombie. From most of these writers I have already quoted at some length, but space must yet be found for the last three, the surviving members of the brilliant quartette who produced *New Numbers*. Mr. Drinkwater wrote as follows: "There can have been no man of his years in England who had at once so impressive a personality and so inevitable an appeal to the affection of every one who knew him, while there has not been, I think, so grievous a loss to poetry since the death of Shelley. Some of us who knew him may live to be old men, but life is not likely to give us any richer memory than his; and the passion and shapely zest that are in his work will pass safely to the memory of posterity." Mr. Wilfrid Gibson's tribute took the form of a short poem called "The Going":

He's gone.
I do not understand.
I only know
That, as he turned to go
And waved his hand,
In his young eyes a sudden glory shone,
And I was dazzled by a sunset glow—
And he was gone.

Mr. Lascelles Abercrombie, now perhaps the greatest of our younger poets and a warm personal friend of Brooke's, wrote at greater length:

" 'And the worst friend and enemy is but Death' . . . 'And if these poor limbs die, safest of all.' So ended two of the five sonnets, with the common title '1914,' which Rupert Brooke wrote while he was in training, between the Antwerp expedition and sailing for the Ægean. These sonnets are incomparably the finest utterance of English poetry concerning the Great War. We knew the splendid promise of Rupert Brooke's earlier poetry; these sonnets are the brief perfection of his achievement. They are much more than that: they are among the few supreme utterances of English patriotism. It was natural, perhaps, that they should leave all else that has been written about the war so far behind. It is not so much that they are the work of a talent scarcely, in its own way, to be equalled to-day; it was much more that they were the work of a poet who had for his material the feeling that he was giving up everything to fight for England—the feeling, I think, that he was giving his life for England. Reading these five sonnets now, it seems as if he had in them written his own epitaph. I believe he thought so himself; a few words he said in my last talk with him makes me believe that—now. At any rate, the history of literature, so full of Fate's exquisite ironies, has nothing more poignantly ironic, and nothing at the same time more beautifully appropriate, than the publication of Rupert Brooke's noble sonnet-sequence, '1914,' a few swift weeks before the death they had imagined, and had already made lovely. Each one of these five sonnets faces, in a quiet exultation, the thought of death, of death for England; and understands, as seldom even English poetry has understood, the unspeakable beauty of the thought:

"These laid the world away; poured out the red
  Sweet wine of youth; gave up the years to be
    Of work and joy, and that unhoped serene
    That men call age; and those who would have been
  Their sons, they gave—their immortality.

I am strangely mistaken if the accent of the noblest English poetry does not speak to us in those lines. And again:

"If I should die, think only this of me:
  That there's some corner of a foreign field
That is for ever England. There shall be
  In that rich earth a richer dust concealed;
A dust whom England bore, shaped, made aware,
  Gave, once, her flowers to love, her ways to roam,
A body of England's breathing, breathing English air,
  Washed by the rivers, blest by suns of home.

[178]

"This—this music, this beauty, this courage—was Rupert Brooke. But it is, we may be sure, his immortality. It is not yet tolerable to speak of personal loss. The name seemed to stand for a magical vitality that must be safe—safe! Yes, 'and if these poor limbs die, safest of all!' What poetry has lost in him cannot be judged by any one who has not read those last sonnets, now his farewell to England and the world. I am not underrating the rest of his work. There was an intellectual keenness and brightness in it, a fire of imagery and (in the best sense) wit, the like of which had not been known, or known only in snatches, in our literature since the best days of the later Elizabethans. And it was all penetrated by a mastering passion, the most elemental of all passions—the passion for life. 'I have been so great a lover,' he cries, and artfully leads us on to think he means the usual passion of a young poet's career. But it is just life he loves, and not in any abstract sense, but all the infinite little familiar details of life catalogued with delighted jest. This was profoundly sincere: no one ever loved life more wholly or more minutely. And he celebrated his love exquisitely, often unforgettably, through all his earlier poetry, getting further intensity from a long sojourn in the South Seas. But this passion for life had never had seriously to fight for its rights and joys. Like all great lovers of life, he had pleased himself with the thought of death and after death: not insincerely, by any means, but simply because this gave a finer relish to the sense of being alive. Platonism, which offers delightful games for such subtle wit as his, he especially liked to play with. It was one more element in the life of here and now, the life of mortal thought and sense and spirit, infinitely varying and by him infinitely loved. And then came 1914; and his passion for life had suddenly to face the thought of voluntary death. But there was no struggle; for instantly the passion for life became one with the will to die—and now it has become death itself. But first Rupert Brooke had told the world once more how the passion for beautiful life may reach its highest passion and most radiant beauty when it is the determination to die."

MARGARET LAVINGTON.

London, October, 1915.

END